SpringerBriefs in Business

For further volumes:
http://www.springer.com/series/8860

Francesco Baldi

Options in Alliances

Valuing Flexibility in Inter-Firm Collaborations

Springer

Francesco Baldi
Department of Business and Management
LUISS Guido Carli University
Rome
Italy

ISSN 2191-5482 ISSN 2191-5490 (electronic)
ISBN 978-88-470-2849-4 ISBN 978-88-470-2850-0 (eBook)
DOI 10.1007/978-88-470-2850-0
Springer Milan Heidelberg New York Dordrecht London

Library of Congress Control Number: 2012949088

Printed on acid-free paper

Springer is part of Springer Science+Business Media (www.springer.com)

Contents

Part II Case Studies

Part I
A Real Options-Based Analysis of Synergies Created via Strategic Alliances

Chapter 1
Introduction

Abstract After briefly describing the strategic motives underlying alliance formation and their theoretical roots and the variety of taxonomies suggested for understanding the phenomenon of cooperative arrangements established among firms in the real business world, we classify strategic alliances into three categories (complementary, shared-supply, quasi-concentration alliances) based on the work of Dussauge and Garrette (1999). We then highlight that the basic inadequacy of the main theories of the firm so far developed in the strategic management literature (Porter's 5 forces, resource-based and dynamic capabilities view of the firm) for addressing the key issues of strategic alliance-making lies in the fact that they cannot properly capture management's flexibility to adapt and revise the alliance strategy over time. In particular, we believe that the need for running a symmetric alliance stressed by such theories does not reflect the reality of dynamic cooperative arrangements in search for sufficient adaptive properties built into them to be able to cope with evolutionary pressures. We thus propose a real options approach to alliance-making aiming at both capturing the evolutionary nature of alliances and advancing our knowledge of alliance performance measurement. In addressing the issue of the intimate connection between alliance evolution and performance, our model conceptualizes and quantifies the option value (or flexibility/adaptability component) of a strategic alliance (value).

Keywords Complementary alliances • Shared-supply alliances • Quasi-concentration alliances • Resource-based view of the firm • Dynamic capabilities • Real options theory • Alliance evolution • Alliance performance

1.1 Strategic Alliances and the Uncertainty of the Economic Environment

Strategic alliances are voluntary inter-firm agreements allowing rival and non-rival companies to cooperate in an effort to achieve and/or reinforce their respective, sustainable competitive advantage. More specifically, the ultimate aim of such flexible and hybrid (in the market-hierarchy continuum ranging from pure,

F. Baldi, *Options in Alliances*, SpringerBriefs in Business,
DOI: 10.1007/978-88-470-2850-0_1, © The Author(s) 2013

market-based transactions to the market for corporate control via M&As) organizational structures is to bring together otherwise independent firms by pooling their tangible and intangible resources so as to reduce the costs of failure of any given project and enhance the chances of tapping new successful investment opportunities. Each partner firm can indeed focus on its core skills and competencies while acquiring other assets or capabilities it lacks from the marketplace. In so doing, all companies participating in the alliance share the rewards and penalties associated with both individual and collective performances. It implies that formation of strategic partnerships requires mutual trust and the intent of pursuing common business objectives.

More specifically, an alliance involves at least two partner firms that (1) are legally independent after the formation of the partnership, (2) make an ongoing contribution in the form of know-how and/or financial capital to the partnership with the purpose of increasing the likelihood of its success, (3) participate in the benefits and managerial control over the execution of the assigned tasks. Alliances become "strategic" when they are formed as a direct response to major strategic challenges or opportunities that the partner firms face. Allocation of resources and distribution of (dis)benefits among partners are arranged according to standard legal rules.[1]

The literature on alliance formation is rich. Several authors have approached alliance formation from a strategic perspective, providing a host of reasons for why firms tend to cooperate by engaging in such strategic collaborations. A brief description of the strategic motives underlying alliance formation and their theoretical roots identified in the literature is reported next. Such implied motives may be classified according to the exploitation versus exploration dichotomy that will be better described later.

Traditionally, multinational companies used strategic alliances as a vehicle to enter the markets of developing countries enforcing restrictive conditions on foreign direct investments (Hood and Young 1979). Although some of these protectionist policies are no longer applied, access to some local markets (e.g., China) is still in many cases contingent upon the foreign company collaborating with a local partner (Beamish 1988; Yan and Luo 2001). Additionally, in developed market economies, firms operating in the defense industry, telecommunications and biotechnology find strategic alliances the most practical way of conducting business in these markets (Contractor and Lorange 1988). In terms of knowledge sharing and transfer, collaboration may be prompted based on a perceived need to access and exploit local knowledge (i.e. market knowledge, distribution channels or more complex government relationships). Alternatively, some firms approach collaboration from an explorative perspective, redesigning their entire value chain and seeking to adapt and learn from local partners in an attempt to maximize strategic flexibility.

---

[1] For a detailed description of common features of strategic alliances, see Yoshino and Srinivasa (1995) and Child and Faulkner (1998).

The rapid growth in the number of international alliances over the past few years has been also traditionally explained as a vehicle for organizational learning, giving partner firms access to each other's knowledge (Harrigan 1985; Kogut 1988; Hamel 1991; Grant 1996). In this sense, the traditional view of joint ventures holds that they are commonly arranged to allow for the transfer of knowledge, skills and capabilities among partner firms (Harrigan 1985). More specifically, most firms take a cooperative stance based on a complementary view and focus on matching knowledge that can be transferred and incorporated in the parent firm. The objective is (implicitly or explicitly) to allow for the transfer of capabilities through the activities carried out in collaboration (Dussauge et al. 2000). If—on one hand—the focus is on matching existing skills and resources, the strategic collaboration can be viewed as compatibility in terms of transfer of knowledge. Explicitly focusing on skills and resources that are needed but not possessed by the firm, the collaboration can be regarded as complementarity in terms of transfer of knowledge (Geringer 1988). Both of these foci are consistent with the exploitation motive. Synergies, on the other hand, emerge from a focus on creating new capabilities through a collaborative utilization of skills and resources. This focus enables organizational—and inter-organizational—learning as the main motive is exploration.

According to Porter and Fuller (1986) strategic alliances can be viewed as a mechanism for hedging risk because no partner alone bears the full risk and cost of the joint activity. Many alliances are shaped around the sharing of risk and cost in that one partner mainly contributes capital and absorbs some of the risk of failure in return for a certain amount of the prospective profit, whereas the other partner performs the actual activity of the joint venture. Reduction of risk and cost through an alliance can emerge in different ways (Contractor and Lorange 1988):

- reducing total (asset) risk and (investment) cost of a large project over more than one firm;
- reducing cost through product rationalization and economies of scale;
- avoiding risks of a full-scale merger or acquisition;
- enabling faster market entry leading to faster return on investment.

Although primarily focusing on economies of scale and cost/risk reduction, the motivation for alliance formation may also be grounded in the need for gaining new know-how and capabilities as partners explore new markets or new processes for product and technology utilization. The former alliances are exploitation-oriented types of partnerships, while the latter are more explorative. Hence, depending on the initial motivation (exploitative or explorative), the outcome of the alliance in terms of cost synergies and learning may be quite different. This alternative potential outcome may lead to inter-organizational learning, which—as mentioned above—is one of the most traditional rationales for alliance formation provided by the literature.

Strategic alliances may also play a crucial role in facilitating and speeding up entry into foreign markets. More specifically, for companies in the early stages of the internationalization process—which are lacking resources to expand internationally and have little or no international experience—a collaborative arrangement with a local partner might provide valuable access to both international capabilities and specific market knowledge (Beamish 1988; Geringer 1988). The development of a successful global strategy and the establishment of a global enterprise is a difficult, expensive, time-consuming and high-risk business (Contractor and Lorange 1988). Forming a strategic alliance may help speed up the internationalization process, which may lead to first-mover advantages (Gannon 1993). In this respect, there seems to be a difference in motivation according to the exploitation versus exploration trade-off, as some firms approach internationalization from a pure economic standpoint by focusing on the most cost-efficient way of increasing international operations, whereas other firms take a more long-term learning-oriented approach to internationalization seeking to concentrate on the entire value chain as an integrated and interrelated system.

The strategic positioning of firms operating within a certain industry and the associated degree of competition may be impacted by the presence of collaborative arrangements among some of them (Porter and Fuller 1986). In an attempt to reduce competition, joining resources through an alliance might help "defend" current strategic positioning against more powerful competitors. In addition, binding existing or potential competitors to the firm as allies may serve to limit their strategic flexibility. Alternatively, a strategic alliance could be used as an "offensive" strategy aimed at increasing competition, for instance by joining forces with a rival in order to put pressure on a common competitor or by vertically integrating into a new market (Contractor and Lorange 1988).

Hennart (1988) distinguishes between scale and link alliances depending on the position and contribution of each partner in the relationship. This distinction essentially reflects different objectives that firms assign to alliances. Scale alliances, where partners contribute similar resources pertaining to the same stage or stages in the value-creation process, are likely to be formed based on exploitative motives as firms seek to control input and reduce excess capacity (Dussauge et al. 2000). Link alliances can be instead viewed as a form of vertical quasi-integration with each partner sharing dissimilar resources and contributing to one or more different stages in the value chain, which may lead to the development of a form of customer–supplier relationship (Hennart 1988). Thus, firms, forming link alliances, are more likely to seek partners with heterogeneous capabilities as the main motivation for strategic linkage is centered around learning and skill-enhancement (Sakakibara 1997).

Network theory also contributes to the debate on motives of alliance formation. Such theory defines a network as a distinct, highly differentiated, heterogeneous organizational form (Powell 1990). Such perspective suggests that networks evolve into multiple webs of technical, financial and social interactions, thus leading to formation of inter-firm collaborations (Kogut and Zander 1992; Gulati 1995). Others argue that alliance formation may allow firms to reduce the level of uncertainty embedded in networks (Kogut 1988; Hennart 1988).

One main theoretical explanation for which firms collaborate is offered by the transaction cost economics (TCE). Intermediate asset specificity and low uncertainty are conditions that may lead to a preference for hybrid forms of governance structure over both arm's length transactions and internalization (Williamson 1991). In this sense, the perspective of inter-firm collaboration has been advanced as an intermediate form of governance between market and hierarchy, which may give rise to strategic alliances, thus suggesting the existence of a continuum of organizational forms ranging from market through alliances (e.g., in the form of joint-ventures) to vertically integrated firms (Williamson 1985; Powell 1990).

More specifically, the theoretical advancements made by the TCE represent the platform for sketching out the basic elements of alliance governance design. Indeed, partner firms may choose between two types of governance: contractual or institutional (Doz and Hamel 1998). On one hand, an alliance can be established through a set of contracts (contractual governance), that is legal agreements arranged by partners on their contributions and future benefits such as the reciprocal transfer of technologies or the mutual use of brands. On the other hand, an alliance can be created as a legally separate corporate entity or institution, such as a joint-venture (institutional governance). The institutional form of alliance governance does not exclude further contractual arrangements (e.g., shareholders' agreements), but it offers the advantage of providing an institutional context for any subsequent contract. Partner firms choose to apply a contractual or institutional form of governance depending on the extent to which it is possible to prepare "complete" contracts, that is legal agreements capable of "completely" accounting for all future contingencies. When there are several complex contingencies to confront with, alliance contracts become too complicated and an institutional governance of inter-firm collaboration is preferred.

Three are the kinds of contingencies that may render the contractual form of alliance governance "difficult and ineffective" (Doz and Hamel 1998): (1) task integration; (2) uncertainty; (3) urgency of decision-making. The more integrated are the tasks assigned to partner firms, the easier is for them to work together via a separate institution. The higher the uncertainty affecting the nature of the business activities the alliance will perform and the markets where it will operate, the more difficult is to govern the cooperative venture via a mere set of contracts. The greater the need for alliance partners to make decisions quickly, the less practical is the use of contractual arrangements without the support of a separate institution. In essence, alliances that require more task integration, face a high level of uncertainty and involve speed of decision-making cannot rely on simple contractual arrangements but need institutional forms of governance.

Figure 1.1 indicates some of the different organizational forms in the market-hierarchy or strategic integration continuum, suggesting a positive correlation between the level of integration and the degree of control. The higher the level of integration (moving from left to right in the continuum), the higher the degree of control. The distinction between a non-equity joint venture (NEJV) and an equity joint venture (EJV) is made in order to emphasize the difference in the level of integration and degree of control, which may have an impact on the relationship between motivation for alliance formation and outcome. A non-equity joint venture (NEJV) is an agreement between partners to cooperate in some way without creating a new, joined entity. In contrast, an equity joint venture (EJV) involves the establishment of a newly incorporated entity in which each of the partners has an equity position. Partners involved in an EJV normally expect representation on the board of directors and a proportional share of dividends as compensation (Contractor and Lorange 1988).

Furthermore, among the categorizations offered by the literature, it is interesting to recall the one that distinguishes between "learning alliances"—where the objective is to learn and acquire from each other products, skills, and knowledge (Lei and Slocum 1992)—and "business alliances" aimed at maximizing the utilization of complementary assets (Harrigan 1985). Such labeling is consistent with the widely accepted dichotomy at corporate level between the strategic choice of exploiting existing resources and capabilities and that of exploring new business and growth opportunities (March 1991; Koza and Lewin 1998). Exploitation is concerned with increasing the productivity and efficiency of employed capital and assets through standardization, systematic cost reductions, and improvement of existing technologies, skills, and capabilities (Koza and Lewin 1998). Exploration is associated with discovering new opportunities for wealth creation and excess returns via innovation, invention, building new capabilities, and investment in the firm's absorptive capacity (Cohen and Levinthal 1990). Firms are likely to search for both exploiting and exploring benefits from their involvement in collaborative ventures. Nevertheless, such a tension between two extremes (exploitation and exploration) should be mitigated opting for a continuum of strategic choices entailing elements of both. Indeed, too much emphasis on exploitation-based strategic choices would lead to the adoption of suboptimal routines, while too much attention to exploration strategies may force the incurrence of high costs of experimentation without obtainment of sufficient benefits.

Figure 1.1 also depicts the above dichotomy between exploitation and exploration showing how it relates to the degree of complementarity (related distinctiveness) in knowledge bases of partner firms and the associated need for control/coordination in order to reduce the level of uncertainty. The higher the degree of complementarity among the knowledge bases of the partners involved, the more likely is for the alliance outcome to be exploitation rather than exploration. This is due to the relatedness of knowledge bases stemming from the inherent homogeneous nature of complementarity. As the collaboration moves toward exploration on

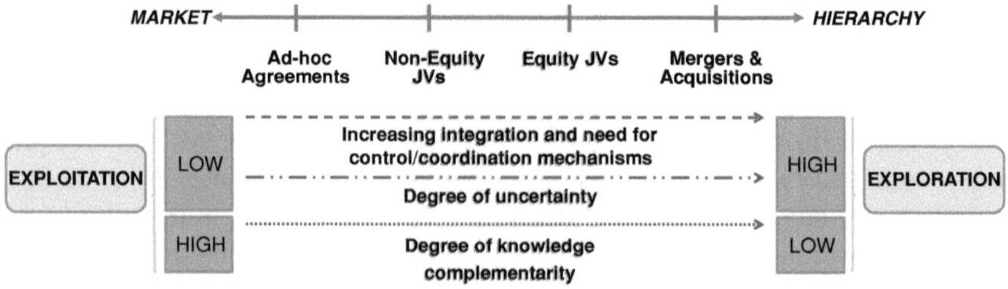

Fig. 1.1 Organizational forms in the corporate integration continuum

the market-hierarchy continuum, the degree of uncertainty increases, as does the need for control/coordination mechanisms.

Child et al. (2005) point out that, despite the variety of taxonomies of cooperative arrangements established among firms in the real business world, there is still little unanimity amongst researchers as to how to classify strategic alliances. For example, Faulkner (1995) suggests that scope, legal form and size of membership are key dimensions for alliance classification. In this respect, Dussauge and Garrette (1999) propose an interesting taxonomy of strategic alliances that are typically formed among competing firms. Our work will be developed making use of such basic taxonomy. More specifically, these authors classify strategic alliances into three categories: (1) complementary alliances; (2) shared-supply alliances; (3) quasi-concentration alliances.

Firms establishing a complementary alliance contribute to the cooperative venture (tangible or intangible) assets that are different in nature, such as a manufacturing plant or a distribution network. As it is evident from the term of this form of alliance, a complementary alliance is made of different but balancing contributions for the realization of a common offering. Core competencies and resources of firms taking part in such type of strategic alliances may be radically different. Allies may operate in distant geographical markets or have different sizes. Complementary alliances are frequent in the automotive and telecommunication industries.

Shared-supply alliances are typically employed to carry out manufacturing or research & development (R&D) activities by equal partner firms that come together to realize products which will be then marketed separately under the respective brands. The outcome expected from formation of such alliances is to achieve for partner firms those economies of scale in the production of a specific component or at a specific stage in the production process that they would not be able to obtain independently. Fluctuations of demand for a certain product (or one of its components) could never be able to reach a peak that justifies the achievement of the minimum efficient size of production for each of the two (or more) partners in isolation. The set-up of a joint-manufacturing activity may allow partner firms to attain scale benefits and contract the size of production costs, thus leading to re-use of the alliance output in their respective production lines or its marketing via their own distribution channels.

The mode of operation of quasi-concentration alliances is analogous to that of shared-supply partnerships with the exception that partner firms typically produce one single good, conduct the related production process jointly and end up marketing it together using common channels. Given the scale of the projects involved and the minimum number of participants required, quasi-concentration alliances may typically take the legal form of a consortium. The aerospace and, more in general, the defense industry has seen implementation of these types of alliances in the past. Figure 1.2 shows the three categories of strategic alliances developed by Dussauge and Garrette (1999).

With regard to the choice of the legal form of inter-firm collaborations, Faulkner (1995) argues that cooperative ventures are commonly established as

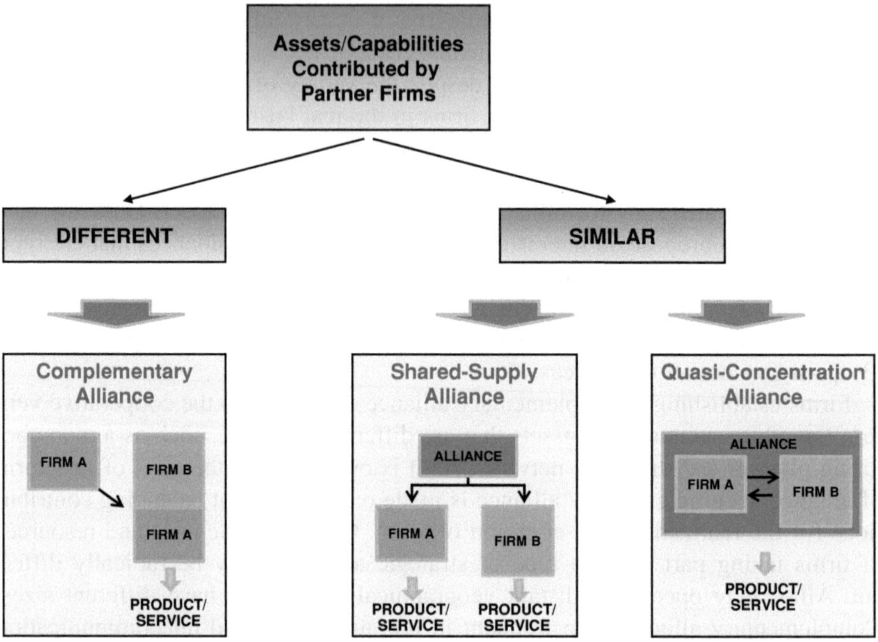

Fig. 1.2 Basic taxonomy of strategic alliances among competing firms. Modified from Dussauge and Garrette (1999); Child et al. (2005)

joint ventures, strategic alliances or consortia. A collaborative venture is legally formed as a joint venture when the following conditions are met:

1. the scope of the venture represents a separate and distinct business;
2. the venture's assets are specific, easily separable from the parent firms, and must be jointly managed;
3. the venture's objectives can be clearly measured in relation to the use of the assets;
4. there is a perceived need to tie in and bring together partner firms;
5. it is legally necessary (for example, to enter a national market);
6. the partner firms wish to allocate a predefined level of resources to the venture;
7. the scope of the cooperative venture is not essential to the core business of partner firms.

Collaborative ventures take the virtual and flexible form of strategic alliances under the following circumstances:

1. there is high uncertainty as to what tasks will be involved in the cooperative venture;
2. partner firms intend to collaborate with high level of flexibility;

3. there is no visible commitment from partner firms;
4. the boundaries of the strategic alliance are not restricted to a distinct business area.

Finally, cooperative ventures are legally established as a consortium when the following requirements are satisfied:

1. two partner firms alone are not capable of providing sufficient resources to pursue the identified business opportunity;
2. a large size is necessary for the cooperative venture to be credible to potential customers (such as governments);
3. the specialization skills required are so wide and varied that two companies may not provide them adequately;
4. there is the need to share financial risks among all partner firms.

1.2 Motivation and Research Challenges

Alliance performance measurement is a puzzle that has not yet found an ultimate solution in strategy-related studies. Indeed, assessing the performance of strategic alliances is not an easy task. Two are the criteria developed by the literature for measuring the final result (success or failure) of a certain strategic alliance (Seashore and Yuchtman 1967).

The first criterion looks at the health of the entity arising from the alliance and measures the extent to which the alliance performs well as an "independent system" (or business unit) by allowing for an increase in the wealth of shareholders via improvement of distributable profit. However, because most alliances are established via informal or contractual arrangements or, if formed as independent entities, are not listed but owned by the respective parent firms and their financial data are typically reported in parental, consolidated statements, market or profitability-based metrics are not usable. Quantification of success or failure of alliances is yet attempted with the notion that the more long-lived the partnership the better. Longevity is typically associated with higher likelihood of positively impacting shareholders' wealth over time. While stability and longer life spans imply alliance success, early termination or changes in partner firms' ownership reflect alliance failure. Nevertheless, alliance performance assessment using such types of metrics is flawed as several cooperative ventures are assigned a short-term goal (possibly, with a specific closing date). This is the case of R&D alliances, which typically end when the outcome (prototype, process, etc.) has been fully developed and whose earlier termination would reflect success of the related partnership rather than its failure.

The second criterion is based on the empirical fact that formation of alliances is mostly associated with the partner firms' needs of reaching strategic objectives at parental level. In other words, alliances are considered as instrumental to the achievement of corporate goals rather than as ends in themselves. According to this stream of literature, a partnership that in reaching its own internal objectives fails to nurture—or even worst, ends up harming—the interests of one (or all) the partner firms should be regarded as a corporate strategy failure and should be terminated immediately. The most practically relevant way for assessing the success or failure of an alliance is thus measuring how the carrying out of the cooperative venture's business operations (with its intermediary and final results) has been capable of influencing the actual performance of the partner firms involved at the outset.

The problem with such measures of alliance performance is the underlying assumption that any strategic alliance is strategically important to partner firms and that its performance will thus be necessarily reflected in parental performance. However, this does not consider the alliance as the sum of the parts contributed by (at least) two partner firms, thus failing to measure the net effect of alliance performance on total parental performance. When a collaboration is complex as to the type of on-going activities and expected results, not all parties may agree on value created at the level of the alliance. For instance, in the case of an R&D alliance, one partner firm may manage to learn more from joint-development compared with the other, thus leading to very different valuations of the partnership.

What described above suggests that assessing performance of alliances is difficult and cannot rely on conclusive measurement tools. Much academic work has been done to seek to understand the antecedents and causes of performance differences among alliances. Interestingly, Child et al. (2005) suggest that alliance evolution and performance are intimately connected. Empirical studies show that a number of alliances end up failing, with only a few of them evolving into long-term collaborations. More specifically, the above authors argue that, on one hand, if an alliance is performing well, it is highly likely that partner firms will commit to investing new resources, favoring its evolution through scope enlargement and undertaking of new projects (related or unrelated to the original venture). On the other hand, alliances that do not evolve into more advanced collaborative arrangements via a change in scope, form or scale may tend to transform themselves into partnerships of declining importance and value to partners. The direct consequence is that such alliances end up experiencing an increasingly poor performance.

More specifically, the academic literature has succeeded in identifying three factors that are likely to positively impact alliance performance: (1) initial conditions; (2) external environment; (3) a dynamic evolutionary process.

First, the resource-based view (RBV) of the firm argues that a firm should invest in key resources and competencies which will give it a distinctive advantage to pursue a set of market opportunities (Penrose 1959; Wernerfelt 1984; Rumelt 1984; Teece 1984; Barney 1991, 1996). In so doing, the RBV shifts the emphasis in the strategy literature away from external factors (such as industry position) toward internal firm resources as sources of competitive advantage. While based on the work of Penrose (1959), Wernerfelt (1984) is the first to articulate the RBV with its initial statement serving as the foundation successively extended by others such as Rumelt (1984), Barney (1996), and Dierickx and Cool (1989).

By specifying the characteristics necessary for a sustainable competitive advantage, Barney's (1991) seminal article contributes to outlining the basic theoretical model and popularizing the theory within the strategy studies and other literatures. He points out that the resources which are rare, valuable, inimitable, and non-substitutable can provide sources of sustainable competitive advantages. In essence, the RBV focuses on resources or competencies as a stable concept that can be identified at a point in time and will endure over time. When firms have bundles of valuable and inimitable resources, they can implement value-creating strategies that are not easily duplicable by competitors (Wernerfelt 1984, 1995; Barney 1991; Peteraf 1993; Conner and Prahalad 1996).

According to the RBV, possession of internal resources and competencies can positively impact firm performance. In this vein, Harrigan (1988) suggests that complementarities in resource inputs and industry relatedness may foster longer lasting cooperative strategies with higher performance. More in general, the RBV's claim is that the resources with which an alliance is endowed with and its partner firms' contributions represent important initial conditions likely to foster the extent of its later success. Among initial conditions of a given alliance indicated by earlier strategic management studies is the efficiency of the original transaction design in avoiding the failure of the partnership due to the opportunism of one or both partner firms. Such transaction cost explanation of contractual features of an alliance upon its establishment is emphasized by the RBV also suggesting that if inputs and controls are properly balanced within an alliance, then the latter will be more stable.

Second, the level of an alliance performance is partly attributable to the uncertainty of the external economic environment (market, technology) where the partnership is operated. Business conditions include the level of competitive forces such as the industry rivalry within the technological domain and the degree of competition in terms of market penetration, or the presence (or not) of government support (Porter 1980; Kogut 1988).

At this stage, researchers have realized that—although the initial conditions of the transaction may be important for the success or failure of an alliance—a static model, such as the one arising from the RBV of the firm in which transactional conditions fixed at the beginning of alliance formation are assumed to drive future performance, is out of date. In this sense, the contribution of the dynamic capabilities view (DCV) of the firm (Teece et al. 1997) has been crucial. Teece et al. (1997) bring the attention to the need for many organizations to constantly develop new capabilities or competencies in a dynamic environment. Such capabilities, referred to as "dynamic capabilities", are defined as "the firm's processes that use resources—specifically the processes to integrate, reconfigure, gain, and release resources—to match and even create market change. Dynamic capabilities thus are the organizational and strategic routines by which firms achieve new resource reconfigurations as markets emerge, collide, split, evolve, and die" (Eisenhardt and Martin 2000). Such dynamic capabilities require that organizations establish processes enabling them to change their routines, services, products, and even markets over time. Organizations are obliged to adapt themselves to changing environmental contingencies.

The DCV transfers the notion that the development and exploitation of scarce, firm-specific resources and capabilities giving the firm a distinctive advantage to pursue a set of market opportunities is the fundamental determinant of value creation to the domain of strategic alliances. The evolutionary perspective looks at alliance success as being tied to the capability of continually adapting cooperative ventures to a changing environment (Doz 1996). Such an embedded capability also becomes evident via formal adaptations of the alliance structure. Alliance is seen as an evolutionary system driven by performance.

More specifically, the dynamic capabilities perspective on strategic alliances proposes that any alliance which persists for an extended period of time will likely develop new routines and capabilities, as selective variations of those already employed by the cooperative venture, for generating new products and managing alliance processes. At the same time, partner firms will learn previously unknown business practices or processes from their involvement in alliance that are fruitfully usable at parental level. The resulting gain may thus accrue to both the alliance entity and the partner firms individually considered. It follows that those transactions leading to the establishment of hybrid organizational structures such as strategic alliances should not be viewed as single points in time but rather as evolutionary processes based on continuous learning and adaptation (Doz 1996; Arino and de la Torre 1998).

What RBV and DCV theories have in common in their respective perspectives on alliance management and related performance differences is the notion of symmetry between partner firms as a key driving force for managing a successful alliance. Symmetry implies that the way partner firms gain from running the cooperative venture should be balanced with neither of the two benefiting strongly more than the other. In this sense, Makhija and Ganesh (1997) suggest that if one partner firm is capable of learning faster than the other, the bargaining power between them—which, with some exceptions, is typically balanced upon establishment of the alliance—could be altered. When such a relative power gets increasingly skewed it creates a growing tension that may cause the alliance to fail. The cooperative venture is likely to be terminated earlier without accomplishing the expected results because one partner firm feels betrayed by the other or, alternatively, one partner firm feels that it no longer needs to be tied to the other via an alliance.

In light of the above, we believe that the need for running a symmetric alliance stressed by both the RBV and the DCV does not reflect the reality of dynamic cooperative arrangements in search for sufficient adaptive properties built into them to be able to cope with evolutionary pressures (Lorange and Probst 1987). Strategic alliances embed an increasing level of managerial flexibility over their lifetime due to the interaction between the set of initial terms and conditions included in the design of the alliance transaction and the level of market and/or technological uncertainty affecting the business environment (volatility). Such an interaction forces the adaptation and re-negotiation of the original transactional terms in the face of changing market and/or technical circumstances, thus driving strategic alliances to evolve flexibly and dynamically.

The basic inadequacy of the current theoretical framework for addressing the key issues of strategic alliance-making based on the RBV and DCV is that they cannot properly capture management's flexibility to adapt and revise the alliance strategy over time. The traditional view of strategic alliances presumes partner firms' commitment to a certain operating strategy. It is as if management of partner firms were to make at the outset an irreversible commitment to an "operating" alliance strategy—by, for example, irrevocably engaging in activities such as selection of alliance candidates, governance mechanisms and time duration—from which they cannot depart, whether nature remains faithful to or deviates from the expected scenario of strategic facts (e.g., market demand, level of competition, technological advancement).

In the real business environment affected by uncertainty and competitive interactions, however, the realization of the above strategic facts will probably differ from what management of partner firms originally expected. As new information arrives and uncertainty about future strategic facts gets resolved, alliance managers may find that the core project(s) around which the cooperative venture has been originally formed allows for varying degrees of flexibility to depart from and revise the underlying operating alliance strategy they initially anticipated. For example, management of one parent firm may have the option to switch to the core production of the strategic partnership via acquisition of the business operations jointly formed with the other allies. Alternatively, one parent firm may have the option to expand the scope and/or scale of its current business by accessing new skills and capabilities through the interaction with the other party. This would enable the former to enlarge parental business operations beyond the original intention of the cooperative venture. Furthermore, a stable alliance of highly interdependent partners which allows for the reiteration of its core project(s) can foster a mutual learning process, thus giving rise to learning options exercisable by the parent firms through a sequence of new interrelated business initiatives and associated investment opportunities. Finally, temporary forms of cooperation may embed abandonment options whose exercise permits allies to rapidly divest shared business operations when the objectives of the partnership have been accomplished.

Management's capability of flexibly adapting the alliance strategy depending on the future business environment changes the perspectives of alliance performance assessment. Dynamic inter-firm collaborations are actively managed and the extra value of their embedded flexibility is better captured if an asymmetry (rather than symmetry) is introduced in the relationship between the parties. Asymmetry implies that some key aspects of alliance-making become optional in nature so as to uncover and properly design those discretionary choices alliance managers are called on to increasingly make in the face of market and/or technology uncertainty.

The asymmetry introduced by managerial flexibility calls for an expanded (or strategic) criterion of alliance valuation that reflects both components of a parental investment into a strategic partnership: the traditional "static" or "passive" net present value of cash flows generated by contributions made to the alliance by partner firms and a real option value. The latter captures the value of strategic (real) options available to partner firms under active management and interaction effects of synergy, inter-firm dependence and competition.

From a traditional standpoint, the appraisal of a partner firm's value to the alliance will depend on the estimation of its present and future likely contribution and will vary in its measurability on the choice of alliance form and the nature of the assets involved. In strategic alliances taking the form of JVs (which are often 50–50 %), estimates are made and agreed on the value of the assets to be contributed to the new cooperative venture by partner firms. An agreement is also made at the outset on what contribution each partner firm is expected to make in addition to initial capital. For example, partner firms may provide raw materials, intellectual property (IP) assets, free consultancy advice, or key personnel to the cooperative venture. All these forms of involvement must be accounted for when valuing each partner firm's contribution. More specifically, partner firms agree to sign off on the figures contained in a 3- or 5-years business plan of the cooperative venture. An agreement is often reached as to the fact that at the third or fifth year of the plan a reassessment is made of all achievements and an adjustment made to the ownership equity or loan to reflect this. In order to prepare the above plan, each of the partner firm's contributions is commonly assessed using a net present value (NPV) methodology.

However, the conventional valuation of alliances based on the appraisal of the value of original contributions of partner firms to the cooperative venture (in the form of the price of the associated equity stake) and its revision to incorporate the effects of the accomplishment of all pre-agreed goals is rather static. In this sense, it reflects the irreversibility of the commitment to an "operating" alliance strategy made by partner firms' management at the beginning of the collaboration, as discussed above. The performance of strategic alliances is instead better assessed if the value of flexibility from their active management is determined via a real options analysis.

Our proposed real options approach to alliance-making aims at both capturing the evolutionary nature of alliances and advancing our knowledge of alliance performance measurement. In so doing, our model addresses the issue of the intimate connection between alliance evolution and performance.

The motivation for using an options-based approach to alliance performance assessment arises from its potential to conceptualize and quantify the option value (or flexibility/adaptability component) of a strategic alliance (value). This does not mean that conventional static, NPV-based tools for alliance performance estimation are out of date or useless. Rather, they should be considered as a crucial, necessary and complementary instrument to integrate an options-based, expanded NPV framework for the measurement of strategic alliances' performance. In complex inter-firm collaborations, an options-based conceptual framework (with associated valuation technicalities) can offer significant payoffs to qualitative understanding of strategic cooperation involving one or more allies.

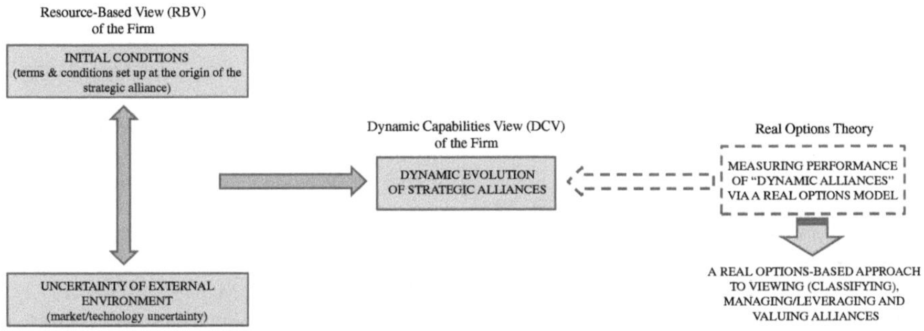

Fig. 1.3 Bridging the dynamic/evolutionary nature of strategic alliances to their performance assessment via real options theory

The role played by real options theory in filling the gap left over by the RBV and DCV of the firm as to how the dynamic/evolutionary process of strategic alliances and their performance assessment (for example, needed for determining further resource commitments by partner firms, or conditions for potential termination) could be bridged via a unified conceptual framework is summarized in Fig. 1.3.

References

Arino A, de la Torre J (1998) Learning from failure: towards an evolutionary model of collaborative ventures. Organ Sci 9:306–325

Barney JB (1991) Firm resources and sustained competitive advantage. J Manag 17:99–129

Barney JB (1996) The resource-based theory of the firm. Organ Sci 7:469

Beamish PW (1988) Multinational joint ventures in developing countries. Routledge, London

Child J, Faulkner D (1998) Strategies of cooperation: managing alliances: networks and joint ventures. New York, Oxford University Press

Child J et al (2005) Cooperative strategy. Managing alliances, networks, and joint ventures, 2nd edn. Oxford University Press, New York

Cohen WM, Levinthal DA (1990) Absorptive capacity: a new perspective on learning and innovation. Admin Sci Q 35:128–152

Conner KR, Prahalad CK (1996) A resourced-based theory of the firm: knowledge versus opportunism. Organ Sci 7:477–501

Contractor FJ, Lorange P (1988) Why should firms cooperate? The strategy and economic basis for cooperative ventures. In: Contractor FJ, Lorange P (eds) Cooperative strategies in international business. Lexington Books, New York

Dierickx I, Cool K (1989) Asset stock accumulation and sustainability of competitive advantage. Manage Sci 35:1504–1511

Doz YL (1996) The evolution of cooperation in strategic alliances: initial conditions or learning processes? Strateg Manag J 17:55–83

Doz YL, Hamel G (1998) Alliance advantage. The art of creating value through partnering. Harvard Business School Press, Boston

Dussauge P et al (2000) Learning from competing partners: outcomes and durations of scale and link alliances in Europe, North America and Asia. Strateg Manag J 21:99–126

Dussauge P, Garrette B (1999) Cooperative strategy: competing successfully through strategic alliances. Wiley, Chichester
Eisenhardt KM, Martin JA (2000) Dynamic capabilities: what are they? Strateg Manag J 21:1105–1121
Faulkner DO (1995) International strategic alliances: cooperating to compete. McGraw-Hill, Maidenhead
Gannon M (1993) Toward a composite theory of foreign entry mode choice: the role of marketing strategy variables. J Str Mark 1:41–54
Geringer JM (1988) Joint venture partner selection: strategies for developing countries. Quorum, NewYork
Grant RM (1996) Toward a knowledge-based theory of the firm. Strateg Manag J 17:109–122
Gulati R (1995) Does familiarity breed trust? The implications of repeated ties for contractual choice in alliances. Acad Manag J 38:85–112
Hamel G (1991) Competition for competence and inter-partner learning within international strategic alliances. Str Manag J 12(Summer Special Issue):83–103
Harrigan KR (1985) Strategies for joint ventures. Lexington Books, Lexington
Harrigan KR (1988) Strategic alliances and partner asymmetries. In: Contractor FJ, Lorange P (eds) Cooperative strategies in international business. Lexington Books, New York
Hennart JF (1988) A transaction cost theory of equity joint ventures. Strateg Manag J 9:361–374
Hood N, Young S (1979) The economics of multinational enterprise. Longman, London
Kogut B (1988) Joint ventures: theoretical and empirical perspectives. Strateg Manag J 9:319–332
Kogut B, Zander U (1992) Knowledge of the firm, combinative capabilities, and the replication of technology. Organ Sci 3:383–397
Koza MP, Lewin AY (1998) The co-evolution of strategic alliances. Organ Sci 9:255–264
Lei D, Slocum JW (1992) Global strategy, competence-building and strategic alliances. Calif Manag Rev 35(1):81–97
Lorange P, Probst GJB (1987) Joint ventures as self-organizing systems: a key to successful joint venture design and implementation. Columbia J World Bus 22:71–77
Makhija MV, Ganesh U (1997) The relationship between control and partner learning in learning-related joint ventures. Organ Sci 8:508–527
March JG (1991) Exploration and exploitation in organizational learning. Organ Sci 2:71–87
Peteraf MA (1993) The cornerstones of competitive advantage: a resource based view. Strateg Manag J 14:179–191
Penrose E (1959) The theory of the growth of the firm. Basil Blackwell, London
Porter ME (1980) Competitive strategy. Free Press, New York
Porter ME, Fuller MB (1986) Coalitions and global strategy. In: Porter ME (ed) Competition in global industries. Harvard Business School Press, Boston
Powell WW (1990) Neither market nor hierarchy: network form of organization. In: Staw BM, Cummings LL (eds) Research in organizational behavior. JAI Press, Greenwich
Rumelt RP (1984) Towards a strategic theory of the firm. In: Lamb R (ed) Competitive strategic management. Prentice-Hall, Eaglewood Cliffs
Sakakibara M (1997) Heterogeneity of firm capabilities and cooperative research and development: an empirical examination of motives. Str Manage J 17(Summer Special Issue):143–164
Seashore SE, Yuchtman E (1967) Factorial analysis of organizational performance. Adm Sci Q 12:377–395
Teece DJ (1984) Economic analysis and strategic management. Calif Manage Rev 26(3):87–110
Teece DJ et al (1997) Dynamic capabilities and strategic management. Strateg Manag J 18:509–534
Wernerfelt B (1984) A resource-based view of the firm. Strateg Manag J 5:171–180
Wernerfelt B (1995) The resource-based view of the firm: ten years after. Strateg Manag J 16:171–174
Williamson OE (1985). The economic institutions of Capitalism. Firm, market, relational contracting. The Free Press, New York

Williamson OE (1991) Strategizing, economizing, and economic organization. Str Manage J 12(Winter Special Issue):75–94

Yan A, Luo Y (2001) International joint ventures: theory and practice. M.E. Sharpe, Inc., New York

Yoshino MY, Srinivasa RU (1995) Strategic alliances: an entrepreneurial approach to globalization. Harvard University Press, Boston

Chapter 2
Managing Strategic Alliances in Good and Bad Times

Abstract Strategic alliances may end up being "good" deals (still continuing successfully) and some others (arranged with the expectation to thrive) may turn into "bad" deals requiring early termination. After briefly discussing the major risks of the (voluntary or involuntary) termination of inter-firm collaborations and the excessive focus on contract design in current alliance formation, we take an evolutionary perspective according to which any alliance should be seen as an evolving, self-correcting relationship allowing partner firms to: (1) mutually learn from their collaboration; (2) detect the sources of uncertainty affecting their business operations; (3) flexibly react to those events that may undermine cohesion and purpose. Our approach looks at flexibility of alliances that management of partner firms can exploit in "good" and "bad" times in the form of strategic options exercisable as what follows gradually occurs: (1) the complex nature of tasks undertaken unveils itself due to reciprocal learning; (2) the internal rivalry among partners shifts outside the boundaries of the partnership due to an increase in contractual completeness; (3) the uncertainty of markets and technologies is resolved due to arrival of new information. Three are the goals accomplished: (1) alliance strategy can be easily visualized; (2) alliance value creation is better measured; (3) design and implementation of an alliance entry/exit strategies are facilitated.

Keywords Successful/"good" alliances • Failing/"bad" alliances • Alliance termination risks • Flexibility • Strategic options • Option-like clause

An increasing number of firms across various industries recognize that engaging in strategic alliances may provide a way to better leverage idiosyncratic resources and grow faster at a fraction of the cost of going into the global market alone. Indeed, strategic alliances have grown at a phenomenal rate in the 1990s with some companies, such as General Electric and AT&T, setting up several hundred and IBM cementing almost 1,000 alliances during the decade.[1] Some strategic partnerships may be structured and managed to become really successful,

[1] In an article from The Economist (2009), it is reported that according to Booz, Allen and Hamilton more than 20,000 were formed worldwide only between 1996 and 1998.

F. Baldi, *Options in Alliances*, SpringerBriefs in Business,
DOI: 10.1007/978-88-470-2850-0_2,

while some others may create new conflicts and difficulties in addition to those that should have been removed via the alliance formation. In essence, some strategic alliances may end up being "good" deals and some others, arranged with the expectation to thrive, may turn into "bad" deals requiring early termination. Table 2.1 provides an illustrative list of "good" alliances that still continue successfully (Panel A) and "bad" alliances that are failed and have been terminated prematurely (Panel B). For instance—as better described later—Laboratoires INNEOV, a L'Oreal–Nestlé partnership, represented the first time that the cosmetic and food industries had successfully joined together to create the fast-growing market of nutrients needed for the physiology of skin, hair and nails. Conversely, Nestlé's management was not equally good at organizing and marketing its innovative capsule-based, coffee-making system in the early days. The joint-venture (JV) originally established between Nestlé and the Swiss distributor Sobal to sell Nespresso decided to assign machine-related maintenance operations and sales support to Nestlé (while its focus should have been on coffee) and targeted the wrong segment of offices and restaurants. Success arrived when the service business was passed on to machine manufacturing partners, marketing responsibility assigned to retailers and target customers changed into households with a special distribution based on home-based ordering through a club membership.

In the light of the high degree of firms' partnership vulnerability, successes and failures are not so uncommon among both leading multinational and small, local companies. Alliances are said to be like marriages, with several firms tending to build a sort of prenuptial contract into their partnership agreement so as to regulate what is to happen to their common assets and liabilities in the event of a subsequent divorce.[2]

In May 2010, for example, Yahoo! and Nokia announced a strategic partnership on some of their core services. Nokia would use Yahoo to power its Ovi email and instant message (IM) services, while Yahoo would leverage Nokia's competencies for its mapping and navigation services. Both companies see it as a way to grow their respective user-bases, with the former hoping to attract a portion of the 9 million Ovi users and the latter hoping that Yahoo will bring a bit of American appeal into a leading global firm worldwide but not in the US market. If properly managed, such a strategic alliance may favor both partner firms. The same cannot be said with regard to those alliances that global companies establish (typically in the form of JVs) in emerging economies such as China and India. Typically, a tight regulation and lack of local know-how often compel companies entering such markets to work with local partners without the ability to hold a complete or even a dominant ownership stake in the related partnerships. The case of Danone, which entered into several JVs with Wahaha Group (based in Hangzhou) in order to pursue opportunities in the Chinese beverage market, is very illustrative. Although Danone held a 51 % equity stake in the JVs, it only executed an artificial control over business and finance operations having assigned only a handful of managers to work in them. The real control of the JVs was instead in the

[2] Source: The Economist (2009).

Table 2.1 Illustrative list of successful (good) and failed (bad) alliances

Time	Industry	Partner firms	Scope
Panel A: "Good" alliances			
1962	Document processing	Fuji Photo Film–Xerox	R&D/manufacturing of xerogaphic machines (copiers and printers)
1996	Pharmaceutical	Bristol-Myers Squibb–Sanofi Aventis	Anti-platelet medicine preventing a future clot-related event in patients with a recent heart attack or stroke
2002	Cosmetics	L'Oreal–Nestlé	Cosmetic nutritional supplements (JV: Laboratories INNEOV)
2004	Consumer electronics	Samsung–Sony	Liquid Crystal Display (LCD)
2005	Telecommunication	Skype-Tom Online	Internet phone services in China
2005	Aircraft manufacturing	SITA–Airbus	Development of a telecommunication service for airplanes
2007	Information and communication technology	Huawei–Symantec	Network security and storage solutions for enterprises
2009	Automotive	Honda–GS Yuasa	Lithium–ion batteries for hybrid cars
Panel B: "Bad" alliances			
1986–1988	Food and beverages	Nestlé–Sobal	Unique coffee-making system (machine + capsules) for the office and restaurant market (Nespresso)
1989–2011	Pharmaceutical	Johnson & Johnson–Merck	OTC medicines for heartburn and digestive diseases
1990–1995	Information technology	Apple–IBM	Programming tools for multimedia software (JV: Kaleida Labs)
1993–2009	Food and beverages	Danone–Wadia Group	Market entry in India (JV: Britannia Industries)
2002–2003	Restaurent chains	McDonald's–Seed restaurant Group	Creation of a joint-fast food restaurant chain
2002–2003	Retailing	Boots–J. Sainsbury's	Boots' operation of health and beauty offer within Sainsbury's supermarkets
2003–2006	Information and communication technology	Huawei–3Com	Enterprise-class routers and ethernet LAN switches in China and Japan
2006–2011	Automotive	Saft–Johnson Controls	Lithium–ion batteries for hybrid vehicles

hands of Zong Qinghou, the founder and chairman of the Wahaha Group. In 2007, Danone accused Wahaha of not fulfilling their agreements as similar products with the same trademarks as the JVs had been manufactured at the Chinese partner's facilities and sold via its own sales and distribution channels. The dispute ended in October 2009 with Danone being forced to sell its majority stake to Wahaha at a 21 % discount over the book value.

Strategic alliances that fail may also lead to litigation among partners. This happened, for instance, with the lawsuit with which in 2009 Onyx confronted Bayer over their JV on cancer drug Nexavar. Their strategic alliance was perfect at the outset. Onyx committed to teach Bayer the art of pharmacological profiling (that is, how to identify effective targeted cancer therapies out of thousands of compounds) also helping to co-develop and test the resulting new drug lead and Bayer had to compensate the biotech company by both cashing out milestone payments upon successful completion of clinical trials and sharing the revenues from future market sales via royalty payments. Onyx bet all of its assets—the human capital of its scientists—on this deal by deciding to shut down discovery on all other compounds, lay off its entire drug discovery team, and terminate other clinical programs. Nothing comparable to the modest costs incurred by the multinational pharmaceutical giant Bayer to enter this project. Despite the agreement reached in 1994 requiring disclosure of research results and patent applications, in 2003 Bayer embarked on a secret program to develop a variation of the compound that the parties first identified early in collaboration by surreptitiously filing patents under a different name and initiating clinical trials.[3] Such a program allowed Bayer to market Nexavar (for the treatment of liver and advanced kidney cancer in US, Europe and Asia, with sales of $843.5 million in 2009) as a direct competitor to the two companies' joint product. Confronted on the issue, Bayer refused to concede any rights in the secretly-developed compound to Onyx. As a result, Onyx decided to sue Bayer claiming that the new cancer drug could be distinguished from Nexavar by only a single atom. The court decision is still unknown.

The major risks of the voluntary or involuntary termination of alliances must be attributed to: (1) impossible attainment of original objectives; (2) severe breach of contract obligations (e.g., due to opportunistic behavior); (3) alliance disengagement, that may result from an unexpected change in the strategic direction of one of the partner firms. This explains why alliance contracts have become more and more complex involving coordination and monitoring as well as enforcement provisions. In particular, recent studies have devoted specific attention to termination clauses and associated exit strategies (Reuer and Arino, 2007; Gulati et al. 2008).[4] However, too much emphasis on the design of alliance contracts may become a risk per se. If, on one hand, contractual complexity is the negative consequence of the rigidity inherited from traditional JV arrangements formed in the past under

---

[3] The compound in question is "flouro-sorafenib", a variation of the compound named as "sorafenib" (marketed as Nexavar) that Bayer and Onyx had explicitly identified together in 1998.

[4] Reuer and Arino (2007) and Gulati et al. (2008).

more static and deterministic scenarios and also the response to the increasing (inherent) instability of strategic partnerships; on the other hand, allies cannot afford to lose any degree of flexibility in shaping their collaborative venture. This is especially important nowadays that are characterized by the uncertainty of the economic environment.

In light of the above, we take an evolutionary perspective according to which any alliance should be seen as an evolving, self-correcting relationship allowing partner firms to: (1) mutually learn from their collaboration; (2) detect the sources of uncertainty affecting their business operations; (3) flexibly react to those events that may undermine cohesion and purpose. Market trends, pace of new technologies, reactions of competitors, behavior of alliance partners, and impact of regulatory changes are all potential motives to engage in or revise an on-going alliance and are all unpredictable. Business environment is so inclined to rapidly change that the key source of alliance instability resides in market and technological uncertainty, thus forcing partner firms to continuously revise the economics of their contracts. Operational terms of inter-firm relationships are often renegotiated; their performance is reassessed; ultimately, their strategy is readapted to new facts that could not be envisaged at inception. In this sense, no one can deny that the *motto* of contemporary strategic alliances is "stay flexible". If this is true, then there is an important question that has drawn less research attention and should instead be answered: "how can alliance managers better cope with uncertainty?" More specifically, "how can alliance formation still be seen as an opportunity to share synergistic rewards and risks in the intensely volatile global arena?"

The basic idea behind our study is that if—the key objective of firms entering into alliances at present times is to enhance their flexibility as to the scope of the collaborative agreement and the resources to be exchanged (*what*), the governance structure to be implemented (*how*) and the number and characteristics of partners to be selected (*who*)—the only way to develop a sound strategy framework for managing partnerships in a fast-changing world is disentangle such a want. The approach we propose here looks at flexibility of alliances that management of partner firms can exploit in "good" and "bad" times in the form of *strategic options* exercisable as what follows gradually occurs: (1) the complex nature of tasks undertaken unveils itself due to reciprocal learning; (2) the internal rivalry among partners shifts outside the boundaries of the partnership due to an increase in contractual completeness; (3) the uncertainty of markets and technologies is resolved due to arrival of new information. In light of real options thinking, we re-discover and refine the foundations of those recent studies attempting to divorce the notion of traditional JVs from that of *new* alliances by placing the latter at the heart of corporate strategy (Doz and Hamel 1998). Alliances are viewed as options and their outcomes are turned into flexibility value accruing to partners, whose potential is increasingly hard to measure. In this respect, the main suggestion provided by these studies is that, as more strategic growth opportunities become available and more choices of contract design can be made, a shift from a simple cost-benefit analysis (of inputs versus outputs) of alliances to a probabilistic assessment of their strategic value would be needed.

We have developed a real options framework to systematically think about managerial flexibility that is embedded in alliances not only formally in the appearance of the variety of option-like clauses enclosed in underlying contracts but also, and more importantly, as the essence of their formation. Real options theory has been already applied to the context of alliances. In this sense, the Appendix provides: (1) an overview of the types of real options that strategic management literature associates with the cooperative stance expressed by firms via establishment of new ventures (typically, in the form of domestic or international JVs); (2) a description (as provided by the same literature) of the economics of those option-like clauses recurring in the practice of alliance agreements. However, what previous strategy studies lack is a comprehensive approach to dynamically managing the various facets of a strategic partnership. Scholars have increasingly realized that alliances should be viewed as progressing over multiple development stages, each involving a different set of contingencies (thus requiring distinct governance structures and, possibly, stage-specific exit provisions) and contributing a unique value to both the venture itself and the single alliance partners.[5] This renders extremely difficult for alliance managers to quantify the synergistic value of collaborative relationships on a stand-alone basis (only considering the venture as it results from the sharing of partner firms' resources) and their impact on the value of each parent firm's business operations uncovered by the agreement. Not to mention the struggle of measuring the synergistic effects of multiple alliances managed by a single parent firm within a portfolio context.

Our option-based approach to viewing strategic alliances may help management accomplish three important goals. First, it allows managers of each partner firm to visualize the strategy underlying the alliance before it is established and its potential benefits (along with the related drawbacks) are fully realized. Second, it helps to assess the value creation and capture potential (or performance) of the strategic partnership by representing an alternative to traditional appraisal tools such as DCFs, cost-benefit analyses or checklists. Finally, it facilitates the (i) recognition, (ii) design and (iii) implementation of an alliance entry or exit strategy for one or multiple partners when the collaboration is initiated and individual contributions need to be agreed upon or it comes to an end and needs to be evenly terminated.

In the next chapters of this book, we aim to provide the key insights about how our real options framework on alliances actually works by endowing the discussion with two real-world illustrations that show how options that are virtually detectable (Chevron's bidding decision to potentially enter an alliance with Petroleos de Venezuela, *Case Study 2*) or formally embedded in alliance contracts (General Motors-Fiat JV agreement, *Case Study 1*) may serve as strategic platforms for better assessing and capturing growth synergies under the circumstances of a happy continuation ("good time") or a gloomy ("bad time") end of the partnership.

---

[5] See Gulati et al. (2008).

Options in Strategic Alliance Agreements: A Glance at the Fiat–Chrysler Partnership

Option-based provisions are increasingly incorporated in strategic partnership agreements, thus contributing to amplifying contractual complexity. For example, in the alliance agreement reached by Fiat and Chrysler in 2009, the Italian automaker—after acquiring an initial 20 % stake in Chrysler—has the right to raise its shareholding quota by an additional 15 % without paying any cash. Such a gradual increase in control is conditional upon the occurrence of three distinct "performance events" accounting for a 5 % stake rise each:

1. *first performance event*: Chrysler gets the regulatory authorization to produce a "FIRE"-type engine (originally patented by Fiat) in the U.S. market and commits to starting its production;
2. *second performance event*: Chrysler collects $ 1,5 billion-worth orders outside the NAFTA countries and signs distribution agreements for some of its products with 90 % of Fiat retailers in Latin America;
3. *third performance event*: Chrysler gets the regulatory authorization to produce a car based on a 40 miles-per-gallon platform developed by Fiat, and commits to making it in U.S.

For each of the above events not occurring by January 2013, Fiat is also entitled to increasing its equity interest in Chrysler by the related 5 % through the exercise of a so called "alternative call option".

Additionally, Fiat has been granted a so called "incremental equity call option" incorporating the right to acquire a further 16 % of Chrysler so as to bring its total equity interest up to 51 %.[6]

Finally, Fiat has been granted two additional options allowing it to purchase the residual 49 % of Chrysler currently in the hands of the U.S. Treasury (9 %) and VEBA (Voluntary Employee Beneficiary Association), an Automotive Union Trust Fund established to pay health care benefits for retirees from Chrysler (40 %).

The first two of the three performance events mentioned above have been achieved on January 10 and April 12 2011 respectively, thus leading to an increase in the Fiat's ownership interest in Chrysler from 20 to 30 %. As

---

[6] Both types of call options (alternative and incremental) are exercisable by Fiat between January 2013 and June 2016. More specifically, the incremental equity option cannot be exercised before the principal funding obtained by Chrysler via the Automotive Industry Financing Program of the U.S. Government has reached $4 billion due to staged repayment. In addition, Fiat cannot hold more than 49.9 % of Chrysler until all of this public financing has been reimbursed. In the event of reimbursement of public funding before January 2013, Fiat can exercise the alternative and incremental call options earlier.

for the first event, Chrysler has started commercial production of the Fully Integrated Robotized Engine (FIRE) in its Dundee (Michigan)'s facility by installing it in the new Fiat 500. The achievement of the second event has also provided for the addition of a mirroring right for Chrysler to access the European market via 90 % of existing Fiat retailers.

Having Chrysler completed the re-financing program needed for the full reimbursement of the total debt contracted with the U.S. and the Canadian governments by June 2011, Fiat has committed to exercise in full its incremental equity call option thus bringing to 46 % its total stake in the U.S. automaker (April 21, 2011).

On July 21 2011, Fiat has completed the acquisition of the ownership interest held in Chrysler by the Canadian government (1.5 %) and the United States Department of Treasury (6 %). After such purchases, Fiat owns a 53.5 % equity interest in Chrysler.

On January 5 2012, the third performance event (the so called "ecological event") contemplated by the Chrysler Group Operating Agreement has been achieved, thereby leading to a further 5 % increase of Fiat's interest in the U.S. automaker and bringing the former's outstanding equity stake in the latter to 58.5 %. To achieve such a performance event, Chrysler has been required to receive regulatory approval for a car based on a Fiat platform or vehicle technology having a fuel efficiency rating of at least 40 combined miles per gallon and to irrevocably commit to begin assembly in commercial quantities in a production facility located in the U.S.

Finally, on July 3 2012, Fiat has exercised its option to purchase a portion of the interest held in Chrysler by VEBA. This exercise for the initial tranche of Chrysler equity covered by the call option agreement represents approximately 3.3 % of the U.S. automaker's outstanding equity. Following the consummation of the purchase, Fiat now holds 61.8 % of the outstanding equity in Chrysler.

Appendix

Overview of alliance-related real options and option-like clauses in strategic management literature

Real option	Description/context	Important in	Research
Option to grow (growth option)	Firms invest in JVs to obtain growth options and sequentially expand into new markets under uncertainty (original, central proposition of real options theory in the context of JVs). JVs provide valuable growth options because, by entering into JVs, a firm is able to both limit its downside losses to an initial, limited commitment and position itself to expand (but only if future circumstances turn out favorably). In operational terms, a firm undertakes expansion by exercising the option to acquire equity from a partner when a positive demand shock materializes	Sequential (or staging) investment	Kogut (1991)
	For multinational firms considering international market entry, JVs are mainly attractive because (in addition to downside risk mitigation) they enable firms to access upside opportunities by expanding sequentially as new information on key sources of uncertainty becomes available. Thus, a positive effect of the number of international JVs (IJVs) on the firm's growth option		Tong et al. (2008)
Option to defer (or wait)	JVs may be used as transitional mechanisms towards acquisition or internal development and termination of JVs may not signal failures in collaboration but exercise of expansion or growth options	Acquisition (one JV partner buys out the other)/internal development	Kogut (1991)
	Internal JVs enable firms to make an incremental, initial commitment to a market or technology		Reuer and Leiblein (2000)
Option to expand	IJVs also enable firms to expand the initial commitment if the market or technology proves to be favorable. In this sense, multinationality and investments in IJVs may allow firms to curtail downside economic risk measured as below-target performance	Business scope enhancement	Reuer and Leiblein (2000)

(continued)

Appendix (continued)

Real option	Description/context	Important in	Research
Option to learn	Asymmetric learning may not lead to learning races (thus only providing benefit to one partner firm) but to divergence of valuations that creates opportunities for trading option rights (thus benefiting both partner firms). More specifically, the more capable party is better able to earn economic rents from the JV assets and is hence willing to pay a higher price for those assets than the other party	Acquisition (one JV partner buys out the other)	Chi (2000)
	Asymmetric learning may be value-destroying if the partner firms are more motivated to invest resources in power-jockeying when they anticipate a substantial wealth transfer after experiencing disproportions in learning		Chi and Seth (2004)
Option to switch	The idea of switching modes in the alliance context is first developed by suggesting that the major contribution to the value of an IJV entry strategy derives from its subsequent, inherent flexibility modelled via an option to choose. If the potential value of a foreign direct investment (FDI) via the JV-related mode hits a certain threshold, a multinational enterprise (MNE) may decide to switch from its current export strategy to a JV. If, later, growth potential increases further, the MNE may switch from the JV to a cross-border merger via purchase of the residual equity stake from the local partner (or, alternatively, exit the foreign market under unfavorable circumstances)	International market entry strategies	Lukas (2007)
Option to abandon	Terminating a JV in uncertain industries creates less value as it pays to keep options open under uncertainty. The value of abandonment options provided by JVs also increases with time to maturity even if they are likely to expire sooner in highly competitive industries. Hence, terminating JVs in concentrated industries (with less competition) creates less value	Equity stake divesture	Kumar (2005)
Compound option	Based on the evolutionary, path-dependent nature of international expansion strategies of multinational enterprises (MNE), foreign direct investment (FDI) in the form of an IJV is interpreted as a compound, complex chooser option. A three-stage market entry model is developed where each potential investment provides information that can be used to improve the quality of subsequent strategic decisions. Phase 1 gives the right to establish a physical presence in the new market via acquisition of a majority, minority or equal stake of the cooperative venture. It serves as a platform allowing the firm to know its local partner better and make subsequent investments to exploit host-country advantages (Phase 2). Phase 3 is associated with two options: (1) expand the foreign market presence by acquiring the rest of the equity stake; (2) dissolve the JV by selling out the stake to the local partner. It follows that the internalization process is not considered as an unidirectional path because the initial choice of investing is influenced by (not only accrual growth options but also) the flexibility to abandon the venture	Optimal sequential investment (with potential divestiture)	Lukas (2007)

(continued)

Appendix (continued)

Option clause	Description/context	Important in	Research
Valuation of option rights	In order for the option to acquire or divest the equity stake in an alliance (e.g., JV) to provide a positive economic value to only one partner firm (and not designate both parties as option holders), they must formulate a divergent economic valuation of the venture *ex ante* or anticipate a divergence of their *ex post* valuations	Alliance agreements (allowing for subsequent acquisition/ buy-out)	Chi and McGuire (1996)
	The reason for an alliance partner to buy out the other is likely to be the existence of a difference between their *ex post* valuations of the venture's assets. Divergence of economic valuations is attributable to greater complementarity of one partner's assets to those of the venture or to partners' differential learning capabilities in taking advantage of the uncertainty over the returns of their collaboration		Kogut (1991)
	In a business environment featuring information asymmetry and opportunism, the economic value of option clauses (to acquire or divest) embedded in collaborative ventures is a positive function of endogenous uncertainty existing over the capabilities or behavioural tendencies of partners. The greater the endogenous uncertainty, the higher the potential for learning opportunities via collaboration		Chi and McGuire (1996) Chi and Seth (2004)
Assignment of option rights	The partner firm having less information (and thus experiencing greater uncertainty) about the value of the assets in an alliance (e.g., JV) may benefit more (than other parties) from holding the right to acquire/divest the venture's assets. It follows that such a firm should be assigned the call option (to acquire) or the put option (to divest)	Alliance agreements (allowing for subsequent acquisition/ buy-out)	Chi (2000)
	A MNE is more likely to hold the option to acquire under a weak IPR appropriability regime. Under this circumstance, the company can leverage the alliance to limit the scale and scope of the technology transfer to the benefit of the local firm so as to assess the latter's capabilities and behavioural tendencies before making any major effort in the above transfer		Chi and McGuire (1996)
Relationship between option right assignment and equity allocation	An alliance partner holding only an option to acquire would prefer its equity share to be as low as possible. Because the option to acquire at a fixed exercise price enables the option holder to leverage the collaborative venture's upside potential, a smaller initial share reduces exposure to downward risk arising from the alliance while still permitting it to fully benefit from upside opportunities. The reverse applies to put-like options to divest	Risk-sharing mechanisms in alliance agreement design	Chi and McGuire (1996)

(Continued)

Appendix (continued)

Option clause	Description/context	Important in	Research
Incentive to include option clauses	Partner firms may be reluctant to explicitly specify option rights *ex ante* under significant uncertainty and imperfect information due to economic incentive problems. If negotiations lead to setting the exercise price of a call-like option clause too low, then the option holder is likely to lose economic incentive to contribute too early because the value of the alliance (e.g., JV)'s assets to the party may exceed the exercise price well before the benefit deriving from the full realization of her efforts. Similarly, if the exercise price of a put-like option is set too high, then the option holder is likely to have little economic incentive to maintain the value of the alliance's assets because the high exercise price already guarantees the party a high return	Alliance formation	Seth and Chi (2005)
	Based on JV transactions from 36 host countries and a US partner, the empirical evidence suggests that the amount of alliances established in the form of JVs with explicit options is 1 % and is stable over time. Explicit call options are more frequent in JVs in which the US party owns less than 50 % of the venture's equity and in JVs that fall into the partner firms' core businesses		Reuer and Tong (2005)
Option-like features of exit provisions	Based on the fact that a systematic approach to disengagement from strategic partnerships is needed to avoid their premature failure, a variety of contingency-based exit provisions enabling alliance partners to set up hard and easy exits—which are either symmetric or asymmetric for the parties depending on the nature of current and anticipated circumstances—is suggested. In all contingencies where the use of asymmetric exit provisions is required the related clauses may be designed to have option-like features. For instance, in the event of a breach of contractual obligations (also as a result of opportunistic behaviour) the "prey" firm may be granted a put option so as to allow the perpetrating partner to buy out its stake in the venture. In addition, when one of the partners changes its strategic direction deciding to exit the alliance, firms may reinforce their right to be compensated through the activation of an asymmetrically hard provision for the exiting partner with the further call-like option to buy the latter's stake in the venture at a discount (its net book value, which is lower than its fair market value)	Alliance exit planning	Gulati et al. (2008)

(continued)

Appendix (continued)

Option clause	Description/context	Important in	Research
Real options-based valuation of options/rights in restatement of ownership and termination clauses	Restatement of ownership and termination clauses commonly included in JV agreements regulate potential transfers of ownership interests in the form of real options that differ from the standard financial options in both the nature of the risks transferred and the exercise conditions (often depending upon occurrence of trigger events). Such option rights may provide an important strategic advantage (with favorable financial consequences) to the transferee/owner, thus becoming valuable assets. Symmetrically, the transferor may be exposed to risks with adverse financial implications. Such risks are of two types: (a) market risk, which arises from the difference between the market price and the exercise price when the latter is determined either on a priori fixed basis or according to rules of calculation stated in the contract; (b) strategic risk, which arises from the transferor's need to reposition herself in the JV after the option has been exercised by the owner. A real option valuation of such clauses is proposed to help parties design and negotiate the terms of a JV contract	Design of termination clauses with transfer of ownership	Juan et al. (2007)

References

Chi T (2000) Option to acquire or divest a joint venture. Strateg Manag J 21:665–687
Chi T, McGuire DJ (1996) Collaborative ventures and value of learning: integrating the transaction cost and strategic option perspectives on the choice of market entry modes. J Int Bus Stud 27(2):285–307
Chi T, Seth A (2004) Exploiting complementary capabilities: a dynamic model of the choice of investment mode. Working paper, University of Kansas, University of Illinois
Doz YL, Hamel G (1998) Alliance advantage: the art of creating value through partnering. Harvard Business School Press, Boston
Gulati R, Sytch M, Mehrotra P (2008) Breaking up is never easy: planning for exit in a strategic alliance. Calif Manag Rev 50/4:147–163
Juan C, Olmos F, Ashkeboussi R (2007) Compensation options in joint ventures: a real options approach. Eng Econ 52(1):67–94
Kogut B (1991) Joint ventures and the option to expand and acquire. Manag Sci 37:19–33
Kumar MVS (2005) The value from acquiring and divesting a joint venture: a real options approach. Strateg Manag J 26:321–331
Lukas E (2007) Dynamic market entry and the value of flexibility in transitional international joint ventures. Rev Financ Econ 16:91–110
Reuer J, Arino A (2007) Strategic alliance contracts: dimensions and determinants of contractual complexity. Strateg Manag J 28:313–330
Reuer J, Leiblein MJ (2000) Downside risk implications of multinationality and international joint ventures. Acad Manag J 43:203–214
Reuer J, Tong TW (2005) Real options in international joint ventures. J Manag 31(3):403–423
Seth A, Chi T (2005) What does a real options perspective add to the understanding of strategic alliances. In: Rauer J, Shenker O (eds) Handbook for strategic alliances. Sage Publications, Thousand Oaks
The Economist (2009) Alliances are often said to be like marriages, 10th November 2009
Tong TW, Reuer J, Peng MW (2008) International joint ventures and the value of growth options. Acad Manag J 51(5):1014–1029

Chapter 3
Classifying Synergistic Growth Options Embedded in Strategic Alliances

Abstract Using the basic taxonomy of strategic partnerships suggested by Dussauge and Garrette (1999), we provide a real-options-based classification of growth option synergies enabled by alliances with indication of the latent real option type and discussion of typical real-world examples. Recurring real options that may arise depending on the form of alliance established with a competitor and are exercisable by the ally include: the option to switch to the alliance's production in the case of a vertical complementary alliance; the option to abandon (or divest) the alliance's operations in the case of a shared-supply alliance; the option to expand the scope of one's own business outside the boundaries of the cooperative venture in the case of an horizontal complementary alliance; the option to learn reciprocally in the case of a quasi-concentration alliance.

Keywords Simple/compound synergistic growth options • Proprietary/shared synergistic growth options • Horizontal/vertical complementary alliances • Shared-supply alliances • Quasi-concentration alliances

Strategic alliances between rival firms are always characterized by cooperation and competition. Past research has shown that alliances are more or less collusive or competitive depending on the category to which they belong. More specifically, as previously described, Dussauge and Garrette (1999) suggest that strategic alliances may be distinguished into three types of partnership based on both the nature of contribution made by each partner to the alliance (to be further differentiated according to the alliance's output) and the degree of competition/cooperation allies allow for *ex post* (namely, once the goals of the alliance have been accomplished). When the assets and/or skills contributed by the partner firms are different in nature (e.g., a manufacturing plant on one side and a sales force on the other), alliances are termed as "complementary" (horizontal or vertical). Typically established to take advantage of the complementariness between the partners, horizontal complementary alliances have the scope to market (less frequently, manufacture) an existing product (originally developed by one partner) in new geographic markets in which the other partner firm has a privileged access. As a firm would have nothing to gain from facilitating the entry of direct competitors into its market, this type of alliance is formed by

F. Baldi, *Options in Alliances*, SpringerBriefs in Business,
DOI: 10.1007/978-88-470-2850-0_3, © The Author(s) 2013

companies selling non-competing or highly differentiated products (or by firms operating in distinct markets). Due to the fact that they ease the entry of new competitors into a given market and increase the number of products available to consumers, such alliances tend to elevate the degree of competition. Horizontal complementary alliances are generally established by only two partners, but the company that learns more from the other may end up taking over the joint-activity leading to a reduction in cooperation. By contrast, vertical complementary alliances are commonly designed to combine assets and capabilities used by different partners at different stages of the value chain—for instance, an upstream activity such as raw material supply and a downstream one such as marketing and sales—in order to reciprocally enhance their competitive advantages. Similarly to horizontal alliances, it may happen that one of the partner firms (because of a learning lead) decides to take over the joint-business thus becoming a competitor to the former ally.

When the assets and/or skills contributed by the companies involved in the partnership are similar in nature (e.g., all partners bring in R&D capabilities), strategic alliances are distinguished according to the kind of their output. Alliances covering only one stage in the production process with the final product incorporating joint-product inputs that are nevertheless idiosyncratic to each partner firm are called as "shared-supply". Those alliances are primarily focused on improving efficiency in production (with no impact on the marketing and sale of the final product) via achieving greater economies of scale on a specific component or on a single manufacturing phase that are successively exploited by each partner in a separate manner. Intra-firm collaboration of shared-supply type is thus aimed at competing with separate, less costly offerings in the future. The impact of such partnerships on the degree of competition is null as their formation does not either increase or contract the number of firms competing in the same market with no change in the diversity of products offered. As they are typically terminated once the efficiency goal is achieved or even prematurely due to inherent management problems, shared-supply alliances have a limited capacity for intensifying cooperation in the industries where they are established.

Strategic alliances that instead span the entire production process resulting in the manufacturing of a common product marketed by all partner firms are referred to as "quasi-concentration". The scope of such partnerships is typically extended to all the main functions (R&D, manufacturing, marketing) of participating companies, which contribute similar assets and/or capabilities to achieve greater economies of scale in the development, production and distribution of the common good. Such alliances are very stable in that they are often operated beyond the project for which they were originally established with partner firms learning to collaborate among each other and increasing their mutual specialization. Indeed, quasi-concentration alliances favor the formation of oligopolistic situations in which competition is lower (with a reduced number of products available to consumers because some of the existing competitors may have joined a single entity to produce only one product together) and cooperation is more intense due to the long-term orientation of the agreement among partner firms.

Synergies resulting from a strategic alliance enable the pursuit of growth opportunities (*growth options*) that partner firms would not have been able to exploit (*exercise*) if they had continued operations involved in the partnership separately. A strategic alliance may allow for the creation of synergies involving new, single investment opportunities (*simple synergistic options*). Synergies embedded in a strategic alliance may also derive a significant part of their value from the follow-on investment opportunities they open up (*compound synergistic options*) (Baldi and Trigeorgis 2009). Similarly to compound options, synergies are interdependent and derive value from the indirect strategic interactions among current and future projects they may create through the existence of the strategic alliance. Under this circumstance, the strategic alliance enables the leveraging ("extension") of all growth options, as long as they exist in the project originally underlying the partnership, leading to follow-on, value-creative investments.

Synergistic growth options embedded in strategic alliances may be of a *proprietary* or *shared* nature (Trigeorgis 1996; Baldi and Trigeorgis 2009). If the joint-business is taken over by one partner at the expense of the other(s) at some stage of the alliance-making, all synergistic growth options enabled by the ending partnership are *proprietary*. In this sense, an essential aspect of synergy valuation, that is the buyer's ability to appropriate the potential benefits of the strategic alliance, comes into play. If the acquiring partner firm is able to develop via learning the capabilities that were originally contributed by the other partner(s), collaboration is no longer needed and the former can easily appropriate the resulting synergistic options. If, instead, both (or more) partners are called on to become interdependent temporarily via sharing their own idiosyncratic resources in order to create a common benefit (with no intent of further collaboration) or permanently based on the ablility to develop specific skills and capabilities in those areas of the joint-project for which each of them is responsible (thus losing their autonomy of competing separately), the synergistic growth options expected from the formation of the strategic alliance are *shared.*

A real-options-based classification of growth option synergies enabled by alliances with indication of the latent real option type and typical real-world examples is shown in Fig. 3.1. An example of a simple and proprietary synergistic growth option is when two firms engage in a vertical complementary alliance. Exploitation of their complementariness along the respective value chains represents a single, straightforward investment opportunity that can be pursued over the duration of the partnership with no need for successive extension of the agreement. Besides, the partner firm that is capable of learning more from the alliance and quickly replicating the skills contributed by the other partner(s) (typically, the supplying company) may appropriate the embedded synergistic growth options via acquisition of the business jointly conducted from the other party. More specifically, the real (growth) option latently exercisable by the acquiring partner firm is the *option to switch* to the alliance's production when market conditions warrant it. The recent partnership between Aramco and Total typically embeds a switching option for the former national oil company. Aramco, not content with its established role as a world raw material supplier, followed the general strategy of all national oil companies of Arabian countries

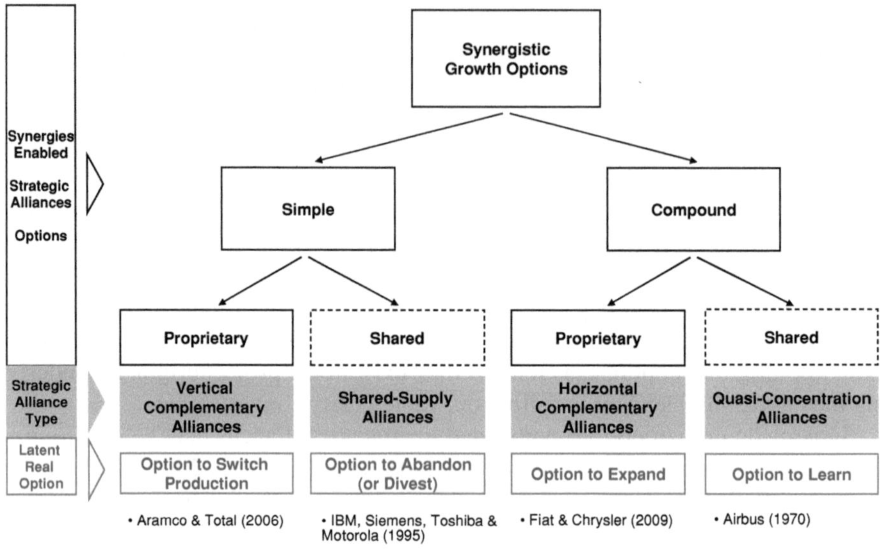

Fig. 3.1 Real-options-based classification of growth option synergies enabled by strategic alliances

to increase oil processing and "switch" from exports of raw oil to deliveries of oil products with a higher added value. For this purpose, in 2006 Aramco signed an agreement with Total for the construction of an export-oriented refinery in Jubail with a capacity of 400,000 barrels per day that further enhances its new oil processing business under development. Such a strategic partnership enabled Aramco to move away from a raw product emphasis opening up the further opportunity of vertically integrating the new business line into the existing parent organizational structure at some future stage. The subsequent integration of the oil processing business from the alliance into the parent firm could help the company control the entire value chain from the oil well to the gas pump and smooth over the effects of abrupt oil price fluctuations due to the greater stability of the prices of oil-based (refined) products as compared to those of unprocessed crude oil with the purpose of ultimately securing additional profits.

Shared-supply alliances may typically allow partner companies to pursue synergistic growth options of simple and shared nature. On one hand, the prospect of profiting from economies of scale in R&D or manufacturing activities is an investment opportunity whose scope is typically limited to the alliance itself. Such partnerships are rarely extended beyond their pre-agreed lifetime because, as the alliance evolves, the partners tend to diverge e.g. on the specifications of the parts to be jointly produced or the R&D program to be performed in cooperation. This adds complexity and elevates the cost of bringing manufacturing facilities or R&D projects together without the adequate compensation of the scale benefits, thus leading to early termination of shared-supply alliances. On the other hand, these types of partnerships compel partner firms to intertwine their specific assets and capabilities in order to achieve more efficiency. Such interdependence, even if it binds partners only temporarily, creates synergistic options that are shared by all parties involved in the same industry via their future offerings once the alliance has been terminated. The short cooperation allowed for by such alliances confers an *option to abandon* (or divest) the joint-business to partner firms.

The alliance formed by IBM, Siemens, Toshiba and Motorola in 1995 is an example of shared-supply partnership with an R&D focus potentially enabling partner firms to shortly cooperate and abandon the venture when the related goals (and associated synergies) have been achieved. Built on both the success of a former high-tech partnership among IBM, Siemens and Toshiba on high-density memory chip development and the outgrowth of separate long-term relationships among the four companies, the new alliance team (also involving Motorola) continued to enhance the already developed 64- and 256-megabit chips and cooperate on next generation 1-gigabit dynamic random access memory (DRAM) device. The semiconductor industry was indeed pushing participants to build up even more sophisticated chips for use in power-hungry systems, such as powerful personal computers and workstations, high-definition digital video and telecommunication systems. The goal of each of the partner organizations was to speedily offer to their own customers the world-class products they needed for a range of applications in information technology, telecommunications and automotive electronics sectors. As suggested by the Executive Vice President of Toshiba Masanobu Ohyama, "the extended alliance of the four companies, each with its own strengths in the semiconductor business and technology, will also provide the platform for investigating new opportunities for future cooperation".

Horizontal complementary alliances embed compound, synergistic options of proprietary nature. These growth opportunities are compound as over the duration of such alliances one of the partners often succeeds in developing a similar business on its own along with that of the cooperative venture. This is due to the fact that the alliance itself enables a firm participating in the alliance to acquire new skills from its remaining partner(s) in such a way that the former can expand the scope of its own business, thus leading to the creation of follow-on investment opportunities to its own benefit. The extra value created beyond the original joint-project may be finally appropriated via exercise of the additional growth options by the partner firm investing outside the cooperative venture. As a result, the type of real option exercisable by the investing partner is an *option to expand* with the alliance leaving the position of the other partner(s) unchanged.

The agreement reached between Fiat and Chrysler in 2009 takes the form of a strategic alliance of horizontal complementary type. Leveraging the U.S. Government's Automotive Industry Financing Program (AIFP), Fiat bought for zero a 20 % stake in Chrysler, the third U.S. automaker with a 12 % share of the local market and a yearly production of 2 million cars.[1] Financially-wise, as better described earlier, Fiat's equity interest may also increase in increments by up to a total of 35 % in the event that certain milestones (the so called Performance Events) mandated by the agreement are achieved, but the Italian automaker cannot obtain a majority stake in Chrysler until all taxpayer funds have been repaid. From an industrial standpoint, the alliance is perfectly horizontal as two former competitors put their complementary assets in common into a new entity (which acts as a "good" company avoiding the Chapter 11's procedure). On one side, Fiat would contribute its technology, platforms and powertrains for small- and medium-sized cars, allowing its partner to offer an expanded product line including fuel-efficient, environmentally-friendly vehicles increasingly in demand by the American consumers under the pressure of the Obama's administration for cutting CO_2 emissions. Chrysler would also benefit from the chance to: (1) renew its too old models; (2) access Fiat's international distribution network (with focus on Russia and Latin America); (3) rely on the latter's management expertise in business turnaround. On the other side, the Italian automaker would obtain access to the huge U.S. automotive market targeting the non-pick-up segment (not covered by Chrysler) with its own traditional (Fiat) and (extra)luxury brands (Alfa Romeo, Maserati, Ferrari) by also complementing its product portfolio with Jeep-branded vehicles in non-U.S. markets. Moreover, Fiat would enjoy both an increase in economies of scale via use of a common platform for manufacturing components for several car models to be sold worldwide and better conditions with suppliers due to the higher amount of orders. This strategic alliance potentially embeds follow-on, expansion-like opportunities pursuable by both partners outside the cooperative venture.

If a partnership is formed among firms that contribute similar assets and skills in order to develop, manufacture and market a common product (quasi-concentration alliances), the related synergistic benefits are compound and shared. The stability of such forms of alliances (with partner firms extending the scope of their collaboration for the implementation of new, completely different projects) assigns a compound mature to them in that they may give rise to multiple, sequential investment opportunities pursuable by all parties. In this sense, new options for synergistic growth arise from the original project leading to further value creation that can be achieved by leveraging the unique set of capabilities brought together by the same firms. The key motives for continuously keeping the alliance together are the high amount of investments committed in the first place by all partners, the reciprocal lack of resources required to stay in the specific business on their own, and the benefits of the learning process achievable as the alliance evolves. All of these factors render partner

[1] The AIFP was arranged by the U.S. Government to prevent a significant disruption of the American automotive industry and the resulting negative effect on the local economy. By requiring participating institutions to implement recovery plans to achieve long-term viability, the program provided approximately $ 76 billion to GM and Chrysler thus avoiding their disorderly bankruptcy.

firms increasingly interdependent so as to corroborate their shared activity permanently. This status of strong interdependence triggers a series of learning cycles with each of them resulting in a higher level of learning, readjustment and higher expectations of value creation on the part of all partner firms (Doz and Hamel 1998). The final cycle typically reaches an efficiency frontier beyond which greater cospecialized commitment, learning and adjustment will produce no further value. Such a phenomenon applies to successful partnerships and more often to quasi-concentration alliances. This equates to a sequence of follow-on *learning options* enabled by the fact that partner firms reiterate their joint-business operations, thus fostering combined growth. Learning options are equally shared by all allies.

For instance, Airbus is not a real company but a quasi-concentration alliance of (originally) four different firms that is perceived by customer airlines as a single supplier. It is indeed a consortium born in 1970 between Aerospatiale (France) and Deutsche Airbus (Germany), successively joined by CASA (Spain) and British Aerospace (United Kingdom), to compete in the commercial aircraft business with U.S. giants (such as Boeing and McDonnell Douglas). A family of commercial jets was developed and marketed (ranging from Concorde, the first narrow-body aircraft, and Airbus A320, launched in 1988, to the commercialization of the latest A380). The common goal of all participating firms was and (under after the recent ownership restructuring) is still that of contributing to development and manufacturing of different parts (cockpit, wings, fuselage) of an aircraft by mutually specializing via exercise of interrelated learning options and forming a new competitor (comprising no longer autonomous entities in the specific industrial space) capable of facing Boeing's domination in a non-natural oligopoly.

References

Baldi F, Trigeorgis L (2009) Assessing the value of growth option synergies from business combinations and testing for goodwill impairment: a real options perspective. J Appl Corp Finance 21(4):115–124

Doz YL, Hamel G (1998) Alliance advantage. The art of creating value through partnering. Harvard Business School Press, Boston

Dussauge P, Garrette B (1999) Cooperative strategy: competing successfully through strategic alliances. Wiley, Chichester

Trigeorgis L (1996) Real options. Managerial flexibility and strategy in resource allocation. MIT Press, Cambridge

Chapter 4
A Real Options-Based Conceptual Framework for Alliance-Making

Abstract We propose a conceptual framework for managing the benefits and risks of strategic alliances where they are viewed as embedding synergistic options available to management of the partner firms. Such a framework involves: (1) mapping the staged paths envisioned for the alliance in terms of strategic options exercisable over the lifetime of the cooperative venture; (2) assessing the incremental, synergistic value of those options; (3) anticipating the potential impact of risks on the success/failure of the venture and associated synergistic value erosion; (4) defining the optimal option map for implementing the strategic alliance via potential, successive adjustments to the initial strategy. All aspects of alliance-making (e.g., alliance strategy or management) are addressed through our real options approach. Our framework predicts that: (1) options to defer elements of the alliance strategy are more valuable when the partnership is established in an unknown economic environment where uncertainty is high (e.g., a new geographic market); (2) exercise of expansion options is worthwhile when the alliance produces asymmetrical effects on partners prompting one of them to a different valuation of intangible assets arising from the venture; (3) switching options are more valuable in automotive, consumer electronics or energy industries, where product differentiation is important and/or product demand is volatile; (4) alliances embedding learning options are mainly formed in the defense and aerospace sectors; (5) abandonment options are incorporated in alliances of shared-supply type formed in capital-intensive industries, financial services, or new product introductions (e.g., consumer electronics).

Keywords Alliance strategy • Alliance management • Internal rivalry • Absorptive capacity • Obligation breach • Real options

Based on what described in the previous chapters, we propose a conceptual framework for strategizing on and managing both the benefits and the risks of strategic alliances where they are viewed as embedding some fundamental synergistic options available to management of the partner firms. In this sense, all aspects of alliance-making (alliance strategy, alliance management, alliance capability building) can be addressed and governed through a real options approach. First, alliance managers that follow

F. Baldi, *Options in Alliances*, SpringerBriefs in Business,
DOI: 10.1007/978-88-470-2850-0_4, © The Author(s) 2013

this framework may operate the process of envisioning and designing the alliance strategy as a comprehensive compound (growth) option, where multiple strategic options are incorporated in one underlying asset (the gross project value of the cooperative venture) and exercise of possible subsequent options is contingent upon that of earlier ones so as to proceed through a staged process towards pursuing higher growth. Selection of alliance candidates, governance mechanisms and time duration may be postponed until market and/or technology uncertainty (the latter case being especially connected to exploration-oriented partnerships) is fully resolved. For instance, following the dynamic nature of alliances, management can *defer* the choice of a complementary partner (horizontal complementary alliance; expansion option) that may allow for the asymmetric stretching of the scope of each partner firm's own business beyond the original project versus a long-lasting partner providing a platform for a durable relationship (quasi-concentration alliance; learning option) via exercise of a call-like, waiting (or deferral) option. Depending on the type of partner selected, the governance structure of the alliance can also be decided as it evolves over time. Equity is injected and a formal joint-venture is established only in the context of research-intensive collaborations, such as shared-supply alliances involving possible joint-R&D arrangements, in order to mitigate the risk of the other partner(s)'s opportunistic behaviors. Less formal, non-equity-based structures may be used for the rest of alliances.

Partner organizations may also have different views as regards the duration of their collaborative engagement. Thus, the choice between the short-term and long-term perspective to be assigned to the partnership can be deferred to a later stage when partners know each other better and have more information to formulate market expectations. The alliance may be short-term-oriented (e.g., vertical complementary, shared-supply) if an exploitation strategy prevails in the face of high uncertainty on both inter-organizational knowledge integration and external market conditions, thus enabling an incremental approach to the cooperative stance and avoiding excessive commitment of resources from partner firms. Alternatively, firms may opt for a long-term-oriented type of partnership (e.g., horizontal complementary, quasi-concentration) in the event of a less uncertain internal and external environment. Under this circumstance, the key strategic motive for alliance formation is exploration and participating firms will have the flexibility to frame their partnership as a semi-permanent entity requiring considerable commitment of assets and/or capabilities and favoring incentive alignment against future opportunistic behaviors.

In essence, the option to defer provides each partner firm with the right (but no obligation) to postpone all fundamental decisions regarding the alliance strategy and not immediately commit further investments (beyond those connected with the start-up of the cooperative venture) in the target market until all needed information is available and the new partnership can be soundly designed. Flexibility to defer investment is more valuable when the alliance is established in an unknown economic environment where uncertainty is high, such as a new geographic market (e.g., horizontal complementary), or in industries with lower degree of competition where the resulting synergistic growth options are shared with the other partner firms in their future stand-alone (shared-supply) or joint-business activity (quasi-concentration) and the risk of their appropriation is very limited. Such an option is exercisable upon the establishment of the alliance at time 0.

Once the first strategic option to defer the design of alliance strategy has been exercised, partner firms have also the flexibility to undertake some fundamental actions for alliance management. Facilitating both integration of relevant knowledge by creating a social space among inter-organizational actors so as to foster reciprocal trust and increase individual motivation to share know-how and protection against unintended spillovers of proprietary knowledge would permit partner organizations to verify whether there is a common ground for bringing together complementary resources to reach compatible objectives under a cooperative stance. If partners are able to form a balanced relationship aiming at contributing, assimilating and deploying "recombined" knowledge, they can proceed to exercise one of the four follow-on, strategic growth options: (1) *option to expand* the alliance scope via engaging in a horizontal complementary partnership; (2) *option to switch* to the alliance output through a vertical complementary partnership; (3) *option to learn* reciprocally via establishing a quasi-concentration alliance; (4) *option to abandon* (or divest) the alliance when a shared-supply partnership is formed. As said above, formation of each of these alliances leads to appropriating or sharing (depending on the proprietary or shared nature of the embedded options) the resulting synergistic benefits.

As a first option, each participating firm may decide to engage in a horizontal alliance because in the future this would allow committing itself to investing additional resources to undertake the expansion of its own business by leveraging some of the other partner(s)' skills absorbed in the original collaborative venture. This implies exercising an expansion option to capture the upside potential in the related market. It typically occurs when the alliance produces asymmetrical effects on partner organizations prompting one of them to a different, stand-alone valuation of some of the intangible assets produced through cooperation. The payoff structure of the expansion option is of call-like nature. The underlying asset is the gross present value of the cash flows expected by the option holding-party in running its own business operations (V). The exercise price is the value of the extra investment outlay (I) required to realize expansion in the target market. If market or technology conditions are attractive to the option-holding party, the value of the underlying asset (V) is multiplied by an expansion factor (e) to account for the size of the expansion and the associated additional value creation accruing to such partner.

Consider, for example, a JV established by a multinational soft drink company with a local distributor to introduce a new cola into the market. Initially, both parties are likely to perceive substantial uncertainty about the local market's reception to the new soft drink. Although the multinational company may hope to benefit from its partner's marketing expertise in reaching local consumers, it is unlikely to figure out how much the local firm can contribute and how much of its own production know-how will be transferred to the local distributor itself. If the market turns out to react favorably and the local distributor is capable of marketing the new soft drink making all efforts to absorb the multinational firm's knowledge and skills, the latter will probably be willing to stabilize the JV in order to also learn from the local partner. This would allow the multinational company to expand its own business into local marketing beyond the scope of the alliance by paralleling the partnership with a separate, proprietary distribution channel.

If one of the potential partner firms intends to gain from the strategic alliance a significant advantage over its competitors by developing extra uses for its assets, it may decide to approach partner candidates down along its value chain and (after postponement of such a strategic decision for some time) engage in a vertical complementary alliance. Suppose an oil company adding to its extraction facilities an oil refinery to convert refined oil into a variety of output products (e.g., gasoline, lubricants, or polyester). This would provide valuable built-in flexibility to switch from the current output to the most profitable future product mix as the relative prices of the outputs fluctuate over time. Product flexibility, enabling the firm to switch among alternative outputs in response to changing market demands, can be gained by establishing and then exiting the alliance by acquiring the business originally conducted together from the supplying partner. The switching option is a form of call-like exchange option, whereby the holding party exercises the right to continue operating in the current production mode for one more period (thus receiving the current cash payoff) or switch immediately to the alternative operations brought in by the other party through the vertical alliance by incurring a switching cost in the form of exit price payable to the partner firm in exchange for obtaining expected future benefits (cash flows) under the new production mode. Alliances with embedded (synergistic) switching options are more valuable in automotive, consumer electronics or energy industries, where product differentiation is important and/or product demand is volatile.

Intra-organizational collaboration with reciprocal learning adaptation of all partners, such as quasi-concentration, creates valuable options to extend such alliances to subsequent products or new projects due to the fact that participating firms engage in mutual specialization by finding easier and less costly to permanently cooperate. These partnerships entail call-like, learning options that management of all partner firms can execute over time when experiencing the series of learning cycles triggered by their strong interdependence and effective interaction (Doz and Hamel 1998). Alliances with options to grow via mutual learning are mainly formed in the defense and aerospace sectors.

Traditionally, alliances are inherently transitional structures that terminate once they have achieved their initial objectives (Williamson 2000). The same principle underlies the real options approach to managing a strategic partnership. Under a real options lens, alliances allow firms to pool risks and share investments at the time of entering into a new market or developing a new technology. Although this comes at the cost of relinquishing some degree of administrative control, the benefits are that a partnership provides companies with a relatively inexpensive means of monitoring a new (market or tech-based) environment while incrementally absorbing skills from a partner. Once the needed knowledge has been learnt and market or technology conditions turn out to be favorable, one of the partner firms may enhance its commitment by acquiring the residual stake in the cooperative venture from the other (single or multiple) party. This implies for the latter exercising the option to abandon (or divest) the alliance. Alternatively, if all partner firms consider it disadvantageous to keep their alliance alive, they may agree to exit via exercise of a collective abandonment option. Under this circumstance, no stake is sold off to some of the remaining parties and the entity is liquidated.

In both above cases, management of partner firms divesting their stake in the alliance may be seen as exercising a potentially valuable option to abandon the underlying project permanently in exchange for its salvage value. The associated claim can be valued as a put-like option on the venture's current value (V) with an exercise price equal to its salvage or best-alternative-use value (A), entitling management to receive V + max (A − V, 0) or max (V, A). Naturally, if the alliance makes use of more general- (rather than specific-) purpose capital assets, their salvage value would be higher and so does the associated abandonment option. Valuable abandonment options are generally embedded in alliances of shared-supply type formed in capital-intensive industries (such as airlines or automotive), in financial services, and in the context of new product (or standard) introductions (such as consumer electronics and data processing). However, abandonment of strategic partnerships should not been exercised lightly without fully accounting for all the costs if such a premature exit might lead to eventual loss or erosion of valuable expertise and other crucial organizational capabilities that could be applied elsewhere in the business or that could prevent the divesting firm from participating in future technological developments.

It may be worthwhile noting that the presence of dormant (real) options of mainly abandonment (or even switching) type in alliance management is consistent with the view that termination is often an integral part of the evolution of cooperative ventures and that alliances may be highly unstable. The strategic motives driving partners to formulate different *ex post* valuations of the venture's (tangible and intangible) assets and, as a result, to early terminate their alliance are at least four: (1) internal rivalry; (2) lacking absorptive capacity; (3) change in strategic direction for one of the partners; (4) breach of obligations from one of the partners. Internal competition is mainly due to the fact that strategic partnerships, as incomplete contracts, lack binding mechanisms forcing allies not to pursue self-interest at the expense of the collaborative venture. No matter what the form of opportunistic behavior partners may engage in, they often attempt to maximize absorption of external knowledge and only give away a minimal part of their internal knowledge. Internal rivalry among partner firms is particularly fierce in horizontal alliances leading to the so called learning races (Baum et al. 2000). Besides, the process of codifying, sharing and integrating knowledge across organizational boundaries is affected by high uncertainty. In this sense, a deficient process of absorbing capacity on both (or multiple) sides of partner firms may take two key forms: (a) poor ability of transferring knowledge due to crucial diversity in knowledge bases, organizational structures and, ultimately, corporate cultures; (b) poor ability of retaining and recombining knowledge, as it is transferred from the other partner(s). Moreover, an alliance may fail and be terminated earlier, if one of the partner firms sees better prospects elsewhere and autonomously decides to change its strategy independently of the successful progression of the alliance towards the achievement of its original objectives. Finally, the end of the alliance may be due to a breach of some of the obligations embedded in the contract by one of the partner companies. This entitles the other party to abruptly interrupt the relationship and be possibly compensated.

In essence, the above first two causes of alliance failure (internal rivalry, poor mechanisms of absorptive capacity) reflect those fundamental risks that may be out of control of alliance/parent firm managers. Our conceptual framework also provides a firm's management with guidelines on how to perform alliance risk management by assessing the strategic value of the prospective partnership and the likely impact of a partner's weaknesses on the alliance performance. The possibility of flexibly choosing the most adequate managerial option (expansion, switching, learning, abandonment) to exercise at a later stage—as information on both partners' characteristics and markets arrives and related internal and external uncertainty is resolved—is a way of overcoming the inherent complexity of alliances (and their resulting high failure rate) taking a disciplined approach to alliance capability building. If managers are able to anticipate the most likely type of risk faced by partner organizations in the prospective alliance, the strategic form (with its associated option) assigned will be the most appropriate to mitigate it and, simultaneously, capture all possible upside opportunities.

Abandonment options may be exercised by management of partner firms against the risk of internal rivalry recurring in shared-supply or horizontal alliances. Exercise of expansion or switching options may be used to hedge against the risk of engaging in poorly stimulating and thus extendable (horizontal) or switching (vertical) alliances leading to lacking absorptive capacity. Before it becomes apparent to partner firms that their alliance operations, if continued indefinitely, may lead to a decreasing capacity of integrating combined knowledge, management may decide to individually expand or switch (after acquisition) to the joint-business. The same risk is prevented by the learning options embedded in quasi-concentration alliances. Over the life of these types of partnerships, it may indeed occur that organizations have not learnt enough about each other to be able to exploit their mutual specialization in follow-on projects. Having decided to opt for a quasi-concentration alliance urges managers to cultivate collaboration through the original project so as to make all future relationships worthwhile. Hence, the speed of knowledge recombination is adjusted depending on the status of the prototypical alliance. Real-options-based risk management permits to create a platform for repeatable success and, ultimately, access to superior growth via alliance-making. For instance, absorptive capacity may be enhanced by repeated involvement in collaborative relations (Lane and Lubatkin 1998; Anand and Khanna 2000).

The real options-based conceptual framework for alliance-making presented above responds to the challenge of developing a new metrics for managing strategic partnerships in the face of uncertainty (Fig. 4.1). Such a framework involves: (1) mapping (and selecting one of) the various staged paths envisioned for the start-up and development of the alliance in terms of strategic options exercisable over the lifetime of the cooperative venture; (2) assessing the incremental, synergistic value of those options (if exercised on the net, tangible and intangible, assets of the venture); (3) anticipating the potential impact of risks on the success/failure

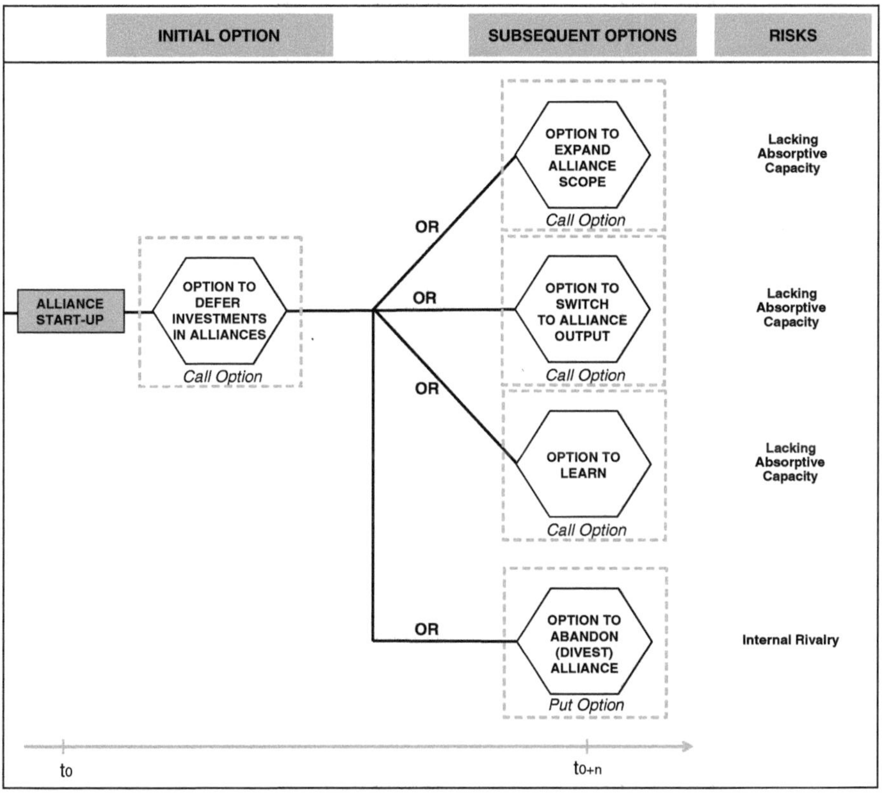

Fig. 4.1 Strategic option map for alliance-making

of the venture and associated synergistic value erosion; (4) defining the optimal option map for implementing the strategic alliance via potential, successive adjustments to the initial strategy (so as to close any information loop).

References

Anand BT, Khanna T (2000) Do firms learn to create value? The case of alliances. Strateg Manag J 21:295–315

Baum JA, Calabrese T, Silverman BS (2000) Don't go it alone: alliance network composition and startups' performance in Canadian biotechnology. Strateg Manag J 21:267–294

Doz YL, Hamel G (1998) Alliance advantage. The art of creating value through partnering. Harvard Business School Press, Boston

Lane PJ, Lubatkin M (1998) Relative absorptive capacity and interorganizational learning. Strateg Manag J 19(5):461–478

Williamson OE (2000) The new institutional economics: taking stock, looking ahead. J Econ Lit 38:595–613

Chapter 5
A Portfolio Approach to Actively Managing Alliances: The SGO Matrix

Abstract We propose the Synergistic Growth Options (SGO) matrix as a tool that combines and extends the best features of the Boston Consulting Group (BCG) matrix and the option features of alliances in addressing the classic trade-off between short-term-oriented synergistic value creation and long-term growth potential. The aim of such an extension is to embed a dynamic, real options-based valuation (current value plus synergistic growth option value) within traditional alliance portfolio management analysis. The economic environment that global firms face is no longer static but it is affected by an increasing uncertainty and associated high instability. Hence, the BCG matrix fails to capture the most relevant upside growth opportunities embedded in a dynamic market while mitigating the severe performance and relational risks arising from too volatile and vulnerable alliances. In this sense, a real options analysis can add significant insights to this traditional strategy framework allowing for re-arranging partnerships into different strategic groups (learning, strategic, relationship, business alliances), which makes it possible to better determine the value of their hidden managerial flexibility. Cases are briefly discussed as illustrations for all types of alliances classified based on the SGO matrix and associated real options are summarized.

Keywords Boston Consulting Group (BCG) matrix • Synergistic Growth Options (SGO) matrix • Alliance portfolio management analysis • Expanded net present value (NPV) • Business alliances • Learning alliances • Strategic alliances • Relationship alliances

Typically, most global companies conduct not just a few but several alliances in both domestic and international markets at the same time (a recent study from Accenture indicates that Fortune 500 companies have an average of 50–70 alliances each).[1] In these cases, the only effective way for managing all strategic partnerships is to follow a portfolio planning approach, such as the one proposed by Boston Consulting Group (BCG) re-adapting its popular growth-share matrix developed in the 1970s.[2] In

[1] Source: The Economist (2009).

[2] BCG developed its allience matrix based on the portfolio approach developed internally by the corporate alliance office of Royal Philips Electronics (Boston Consulting Group Report 2005).

F. Baldi, *Options in Alliances*, SpringerBriefs in Business,
DOI: 10.1007/978-88-470-2850-0_5,

this BCG matrix, each alliance is mapped on a two-dimensional grid. One dimension represents the alliance's profitability measured by the amount of synergies expected to be generated between the partner firms (which corresponds to the ROA or market share in the original matrix). The other dimension reflects the potential long-term value of the alliance to one of the parent companies (the one analyzing the partnership via the matrix), which substitutes for real market growth in the original matrix. Thus, the BCG matrix categorizes alliances into four quadrants. Strategic alliances are the equivalent of "question marks" (of the popular BCG matrix) and are defined as those partnerships with low synergy but prospects of high long-term value. They are aimed at creating new products, services, or business lines. Proper cultivation through additional investments may turn these partnerships into corporate alliances ("rising stars") that are particularly important for achieving the strategic goals of the parent company due to their high immediate profitability in terms of synergies and great long-term value contribution. Relationship alliances—which correspond to long-lasting partnerships usually spanning multiple divisions—are analogous to "cash cows" as they are nurtured in stable or declining markets with relatively solid synergy-based value creation. Finally, business alliances—that have an operational scope mainly focused on logistics or purchasing—are low-profit partnerships in slow-growth markets, and, similarly to what happens for "dogs", are to be avoided or divested.

Management of partner firms may use this matrix for the active management of their portfolio of alliances in a relatively stable and certain environment. Such a portfolio management approach recommends that companies make use of the synergistic value created (in the form of cash flows) from relationship alliances to further explore strategic alliances and develop more corporate alliances. That is, one should balance exploitation and exploration.

However, the economic environment that global firms face is no longer static but it is indeed affected by an increasing uncertainty and associated high instability. Hence, the above BCG matrix may fail to capture the most relevant upside growth opportunities embedded in a dynamic market while mitigating the severe performance and relational risks arising from too volatile and vulnerable alliances. In this sense, a real options analysis can add significant insights to this traditional strategy framework enabling to re-arrange partnerships into different strategic groups, which makes it possible to better determine the value of their hidden managerial flexibility. Additional investment into existing (or even prospective) alliances only becomes necessary if internal and/or external uncertainty continues to resolve itself favorably. This permits not to perform alliance-making in a static scenario, but to actively and dynamically react to internal knowledge adaptation and external market developments by making the most proper adjustments to the strategic design and management of on-going partnerships.

We then propose the Synergistic Growth Options (SGO) matrix as a tool that combines and extends the best features of the BCG matrix and the option features of alliances described above in addressing the classic trade-off between short-term-oriented synergistic value creation and long-term growth potential (Fig. 5.1, Panel A). Our matrix proposes that alliances, formed by a firm over time and managed with a portfolio view, be represented along two dimensions of value.

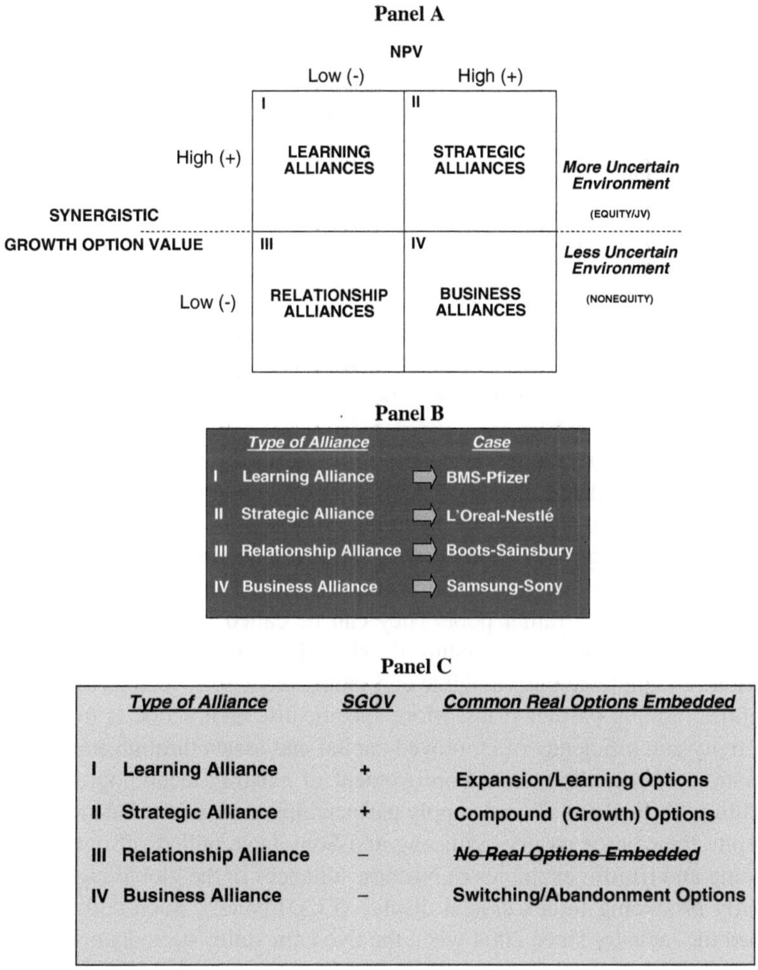

Fig. 5.1 Synergistic Growth Options (SGO) matrix

The horizontal axis measures the direct NPV (or net present value) component of alliance value, capturing present profitability from immediate synergies. The vertical axis measures the present value of those future synergistic options that, if embedded in alliances, can be actively exercised by management of partner firms to further enhance growth. This latter dimension, which corresponds to the value of the alliance's real (growth) options, combines both volatility and adaptability. The aim of such an extension of the BCG matrix presented here via the SGO matrix is to embed a dynamic, real options-based valuation (current value plus synergistic growth option value) within traditional alliance portfolio management analysis. To operationalize a real options analysis of alliances, we recast the expanded NPV criterion developed within real options theory to assess to what extent, for instance, an alliance formed between firm A and firm B derives its strategic value from (hidden, still unexploited) managerial flexibility. At any stage of alliance development, total value creation expected from continuation of the alliance can thus be viewed as the sum of the cash flows from immediately exploitable synergies when A is allied with B (net present value, NPV) plus an additional component capturing potential growth opportunities (synergistic growth option value, SGOV) that, if identified and properly nurtured, partner organizations A and B can pursue in the near future. The general formula is:

$$\text{expanded NPV of Alliance (A+B)} = \text{NPV} + \text{Value of Synergistic Growth Options.}$$

While NPV is conventionally measured, SGOV can be estimated using option valuation methods based on identification of individual options embedded in the alliance (according to the classification provided in Fig. 3.1), determination of their parameters and pricing.

In the SGO matrix, a firm's alliances may fall in different quadrants based on their current NPV-related synergy versus relative synergistic growth option value potential. The bottom-right of the SGO matrix (quadrant IV) comprises alliances with low synergistic growth option potential that are formed and maintained mostly for cash generation from immediate synergies. Indeed, their prospective strategic growth option value is rather poor. They can be called *business alliances*, which are exploitation-oriented partnerships in that they are aimed at optimizing the utilization of complementary tangible and intangible assets, such as equipment and capabilities, among partner firms. More specifically, their scope is to increase the productivity and efficiency of employed capital and assets through standardization, systematic cost reductions, and improvement of existing technologies, skills, and capabilities. Vertical and shared-supply partnerships are types of business alliances.

Despite their fierce rivalry, Samsung and Sony have pulled off one of the most interesting and fruitful examples of business alliances in the global high-tech sector by jointly producing liquid–crystal display (LCD) panels. Such collaboration has reshaped the industry since 2004 when the two companies started working together on the technology. Sony dispatched its own engineers to the joint venture to vet LCD displays insisting that every panel had to be shipped through its LCD-TV factory to perform quality tests. While the engineering and production has been a success for Sony, Samsung's own LCD-TV business has made big strides. Samsung has indeed emerged as a trend-setter in the LCD-panel industry with the aid of Sony's technology that has helped ensure high-quality and sharp TV pictures. Nonetheless, the business in which the two partner firms operate is subject to continuous innovation and as new technologies are brought to light, LCD era is deemed to vanish. This implies that while the NPV of the Samsung-Sony alliance is high and must be rapidly captured before a disruptive innovation is introduced, the synergistic growth option value of such collaboration is close to zero.

In the diagonally opponent, top-left region of the SGO matrix (quadrant I), synergistic growth option value rises at the expense of the immediate (lower or negative) NPV. Such quadrant hosts what we call *learning alliances* that are currently unprofitable but have high growth option potential. These partnerships present high innovation content and are at a stage of their life-cycle in which they have not yet proven themselves in the marketplace. Their exploration-oriented objective is to let partner firms learn and acquire from each other products, skills, and knowledge. Learning alliances are commonly used to discover new growth opportunities for value creation outside organizational boundaries via innovation, invention, and investment in the absorptive capacity of all partners involved. Horizontal and quasi-concentration partnerships represent forms of learning alliances, as they allow one or all partner firms to create an extension of the original joint-business based on exclusive or mutual learning.

One example of a learning alliance is given by the strategic agreement in which Bristol-Myers-Squibb (BMS) and Pfizer entered in the second quarter of 2007. The aim of such agreement was to further develop and commercialize an oral anticoagulant compound named Apixaban that BMS had discovered earlier. The two partner firms have successfully developed a product which appears to be superior to all others proposed by competitors and represents a breakthrough in the related field. This successful agreement between Pfizer and BMS has, over time, laid roots for a set of further collaborations. Not only the two companies are still active on the development and improvement of the anticoagulant but they are also jointly working on the research, development and commercialization of a Pfizer's discovery program, which includes preclinical compounds with potential applications for the treatment of metabolic disorders (e.g. diabetes).

Alliances that are positioned in the top-right region of the SGO matrix (quadrant II) are currently in-the-money (NPV > 0) but may be even more valuable to the parent entities of partner firms if cultivated and better exploited later. Indeed, the synergistic growth option value potential of the so called *strategic alliances* is so high that, if partner firms invest additional resources to foster a positive interaction among the assets and capabilities they have respectively contributed to the alliance, they would be able to well-match their stand-alone knowledge bases by optimally recombining and deploying them for exploitation or exploration purposes in a complementary and cooperative manner. Such a perfect match of fully integrated skills, competences and capabilities may become a strategic platform for opening up further avenues for growth. In other words, more synergies can be extracted by partner firms if the *core* project underlying the original formation of the alliance is no longer looked at as an independent investment, but rather as the first link in a chain of follow-on, interrelated growth opportunities. Alliance development involves a process analogous to exercising a sequence of strategically relevant, synergistic options that could not be exercised if the partnership had not been established in the first place. Alliances grouped in this region of the SGO matrix have, more than others, typical compound (growth) option characteristics. For instance, a collaboration originally established for developing a first-generation technology or a new drug with multiple extensions may not only deliver immediate cash flows from current exploitation of core business but also bring additional strategic value to partner firms in the form of (potentially valuable) synergistic options associated with interrelated projects, whose future exercise could further propel the growth of the cooperative venture.

In June 2002 L'Oreal, the cosmetics giant, and Nestlé, the world's largest food company, created a joint venture named Laboratories INNEOV, which has become an excellent example of a strategic alliance. This collaboration has been put up in order to pioneer the nutriocosmetics business. The two companies have shared their strong know-how on nutrition and cosmetics to research on and develop products aimed at skin, hair and nails care. Based on a successful integration of very different expertise contributed by the two partner firms, INNEOV has developed and currently markets a set of products operating in the completely new and growing market of "beauty pills". Because the joint venture—which currently sells in 16 European countries, in Brazil and Mexico—plans to enter China and other countries of Latin America as more people turn to dietary supplements to treat skin and hair conditions, the value of the cooperative venture is not merely limited to the NPV of channeling the same products in new geographic markets. More importantly, its value derives from the synergistic options that the knowledge sharing carried out by the two partner firms may open up if new R&D efforts are jointly made moving forward along the lines of the needs expressed by consumers' demand. The two partner firms have the competitive advantage of being currently alone in knowing and serving the market. The value potential of such pioneering market, which L'Oreal and Nestlé have contributed to invent, lies in the combination of expertise buildup and market knowledge that may be promptly exploited to respond to new market needs.

Finally, alliances in the bottom-left quadrant (III) of the matrix having both low direct NPV and low synergistic growth option value should be abandoned via divesture. These partnerships are named as *relationship alliances*, because they are the result of an unfruitful (perhaps even long-lasting) liaison with some other competing or non-competing organizations that has been unable to evolve into a valuable, growth-fostering alliance. For instance, relationship alliances may be formed with the purpose of gaining, at the level of the parent entities, cost synergies through consolidation and restructuring or launching a marketing initiative. Nevertheless, if the underlying project or idea is unable to create immediate (NPV-based) value creation potential and, more importantly, lacks adaptive capabilities to react to a rapidly changing environment, then the alliance—though based on a strong inter-firm relationship originated beforehand—would not long survive. This is the case of the engagement of Boots and Sainsbury in a health and beauty joint venture that lasted only 16 months between 2002 and 2003.

The idea to offer Boots' products and services within Sainsbury's shops was originated by Mr. Russell, the CEO of Boots who had worked at the company since 1967. He came up with the idea and approached Sir Peter Davis, the CEO of Sainsbury, with it. The two men knew each other well, since Sir Davis had been a non-executive director of Boots for eight years before re-joining Sainsbury. The trial began in October 2001 and at that time Mr. Russell talked of the possibility of opening Boots shops in up to 100 Sainsbury's supermarkets. There was even speculation that it might eventually lead to a merger between the two companies, although Mr. Russell always publicly dismissed that idea. Concretely, the alliance took place in nine of Sainsbury's supermarkets, where Boots was allowed to manage its own shops. Nonetheless, the two companies had to step back and abort their initiative having to face write-offs up to 10 million pounds. Sir Peter Davis said: "We could not reach terms that both sides were happy with for sharing the value. We always said we would set sales and profits targets, but we did not achieve a level sufficient to have enough to share between the two companies".

Relationship and business alliances are more prone to be formed and prosper in less uncertain environments. Learning and strategic alliances are more adapt to respond to the challenges of more uncertain and volatile environments. It follows that the former are typically structured as non-equity alliances with less coordination and control mechanisms in place, while the latter may take the form of equity-based alliances or joint-ventures involving more hierarchy. Business alliances of shared-supply type, learning and strategic alliances tend to adopt a shared approach to joint-management whereby both (or all) parties are active participants. Nevertheless, if learning and strategic alliances are structured in the form of JVs, the creation of a new entity that is legally distinct from its parent firms may also induce the arrangement of a delegated approach to jointly managing the underlying business with a responsible task-splitting among the managerial teams brought by each of them. Finally, business alliances of vertical complementary nature may see one partner (typically the supplying partner) take a primary responsibility in the development of the joint-project (with the possibility for the demanding partner to rapidly learn from the ally and acquire the alliance business). This type of alliance management scheme is called assigned arrangement.

The cases provided above as illustrations for all types of alliances classified based on the Synergistic Growth Options (SGO) matrix are summarized in Fig. 5.1, Panel B. The real options incorporated in all types of alliances classified based on the SGO matrix are summarized in Fig. 5.1, Panel C.

With our SGO matrix, management can project a portfolio of alliances into the future, developing a trajectory that starts with maximizing the number of business alliances to inject investment capital into learning alliances and, ultimately, turn them into strategic alliances. In the first place, firms should then be capable of well balancing their portfolios of alliances to rapidly exercise switching and abandonment options embedded in business alliances to squeeze current synergies.

Value (and associated cash) may be easily generated at parental level by vertically integrating the business activity originally assigned to the alliance (of complementary type) and internalizing the efficiency gains obtained via exploitation and subsequent divestiture of a shared-supply partnership. This typically occurs when the objective of the partnership is achieved allowing one partner firm to "learn and go" by paying (or receiving) a price to (from) the other party. In the case of vertical integration, one ally pays the purchase price to acquire (from the other) the alliance-based activity and access synergistic growth from incorporating it into the pre-existing business so as to stretch the latter out along the value chain. Such a move corresponds to the exercise of a switching option. In the case of termination of a shared-supply alliance, based upon the fact that the economies of scale at production and/or process level have been fully realized, one ally divests to receive the fair value of its equity stake in the cooperative venture from the partner firm. The former party decides to abandon the alliance so as to benefit from efficiency gains in its own separate manufacturing activities. This decision equates to the exercise of an abandonment option.

Cash created from management of business alliances and timely exercise of embedded real options may be then used to foster learning alliances. A parent company may allocate the financial resources generated via business alliances in its own portfolio to the promotion, establishment and execution of those partnerships, such as horizontal complementary and quasi-concentration alliance, featuring low short-term value and high future growth options potential. Such collaborative ventures are defined as learning alliances in that partner firms involved are in a better position of accessing other parties' knowledge, thus improving their own skills and competencies. Typically, the condition of parity among partners implied by a horizontal venture—where each ally contributes different but equally important tangible or intangible assets—and a quasi-concentration arrangement—where all partners are challenged by the task of more efficiently producing a common (pre-existing or new) output via pooling similar inputs with lower single risk exposure—enables reciprocal learning.

In the first type of alliance (horizontal complementary), those partners that are faster at learning may profit from the integration of the shared business at parental level in exchange for the payment of the selling price to the ally (or allies) not interested in keeping the cooperative venture alive or appropriating the related activity. This equates to exercising an option to expand the organizational boundaries of the parent company by paying the investment cost (as exercise price) required for the realization of an optimal integration. Expansion of the scope of the current business area based on generation of new, interlinked growth opportunities has the potential to create extra value. Such opportunities take the form of subsequent options whose timely exercise enables the parent company to grow incrementally and secure the resulting value creation.

In the second form of alliance (quasi-concentration), stability and interdependence of the collaboration among partner firms promote a collection of learning options which, if nurtured in a shared manner and properly exercised at individual level but with the common agreement of all allies, can strengthen the partnership and transform it into a competing entity in the business arena. In facing market demand and negotiating with suppliers, the alliance—although it is made of a diversified group of individual companies—behaves like a compacted, stand-alone party. More than in the context of the other types of alliances, relative absorptive capacity and internal rivalry become two antagonist sides of the same coin. While fighting internally for the control of the cooperative venture, partner firms of a quasi-concentration alliance seek to accomplish the common goal of capturing the value of common synergies via exercise of long-term, synergistic growth options.

Finally, it should be taken into account that both expansion and learning options embedded in horizontal and quasi-concentration alliances have a compound nature. Such characteristic is very important as it represents the platform for converting inter-firm collaborations of learning type into strategic alliances. If—as the alliance evolves dynamically by adapting itself to the changing business environment—management of partner firms are able to identify, nurture and (only if it is optimal to do so) exercise a sequence of follow-on, interrelated growth options, then the collaborative venture becomes a strategic alliance. Interaction and reconfiguration of physical and intangible resources among partner firms is so prolific that the project (or the set of projects) around which the alliance has been initially established is no longer viewed and valued in isolation but as the origin of a chain of intertwined options. Exercise of such options drives growth easily transferable from the level of partner firms to that of corporate parents.

For this reason, strategic alliances should play the most important role in the alliance portfolio of a firm. They should be assigned an adequate amount of financial resources, partially created via the mechanism described above which consists of (1) extracting synergistic option value from leveraging business alliances and (2) allocating a proportion of the funds created into development of learning alliances. Flexible adaptation of partner firms to the changing market and technological landscape permits their alliance to dynamically evolve via optimal exercise of compound (growth) options. The value creation path resulting from the alliance-related, synergistic option portfolio strategy described herein demonstrates that alliance management and their performance valuation are strongly interconnected and that their intimate intertwine may be better understood if viewed through real options lens.

References

Cools K, Roos A (2005) The role of alliances in corporate strategy. The Boston Consulting Group Report. Nov 2005

The Economist (2009) Alliances are often said to be like marriages, 10th Nov 2009

Chapter 6
Conclusions

Abstract We propose a dynamic view of inter-firm collaborations that disciplines the acceptable normative prescriptions provided by the theory of strategic management via a more rigorous analytical process to help alliance managers cultivate and exploit long-run adaptive flexibility and, as a result, create and sustain competitive advantage. Our options-approach to strategic alliance-making brings coherently together the key paradigms developed in the strategy literature into a single, comprehensive framework. In line with the resource-based view of the firm, strategic growth options should be exercised with reference to the competences and capabilities that the alliance has relative to its competitors. Consistently with the dynamic capabilities view of the firm, an alliance strategy can be seen as a series of long-term, partly irreversible commitments to certain domains of competence, which is similar to a chain of interrelated strategic (compound-like) options whose exercise accumulates resources over time and generates new opportunities in an uncertain environment. Hence, options thinking enables an explicit quantification of alliance strategy under uncertainty, which encompasses NPV analysis as a special case and incorporates the value of real options arising from management of evolving cooperative ventures. It represents an alternative methodology for estimating the "real" performance of a strategic partnership if compared to traditional tools (e.g., cost-benefit analysis, DCF).

Keywords Competitive forces approach • Resource-based view of the firm • Dynamic capabilities • Competitive advantage • NPV analysis • Managerial flexibility • Real options

In the current highly volatile and competitive business environment, the horizon over which the performance of strategic alliances can be appraised confidently is shrinking, making it crucial for partner firms to be more flexible in their investment programs. The future is uncertain, and as the alliance's dynamic evolution path unfolds, partner firms' management can learn, adapt, and revise future investment decisions in response to unexpected market or technology developments.

F. Baldi, *Options in Alliances*, SpringerBriefs in Business,
DOI: 10.1007/978-88-470-2850-0_6, © The Author(s) 2013

An estimation of the value impact (at parental level) of inter-firm collaborative arrangements in a dynamic environment has become more complicated than standard tools—such as cost-benefit analysis, strategic assessment, net present value (NPV) or discounted cash-flow (DCF) methodologies—may typically suggest. Indeed, the latter techniques implicitly assume a static view of alliance development and its embedded investment decisions, where the initial terms of the partnership influence its future performance and no revision of rules/conditions/plans is possible as market or operational uncertainty gets resolved. In this context, a real options framework adds a dynamic perspective to the traditional alliance planning and appraisal approach by better linking evolution to performance of strategic partnerships through incorporating and properly quantifying the value of managerial flexibility and growth opportunities associated with cooperative ventures over their entire lifetime.

The options-approach to managing and valuing strategic alliances presented here brings coherently together the key paradigms—such as the competitive analysis based on Porter's five forces, the resource-based and the dynamic capabilities views of the firm—previously developed in the strategy literature into a single, comprehensive framework.

The above strategic management theories (competitive forces approach, RBV and DCV) provide a different view of whether the sources of competitive advantage and value creation of cooperative arrangements among firms are internal or external to partners. However, none of them is alone capable of capturing the evolutionary and non-symmetric nature of current dynamic alliances. All of them are based on the conventional notion that partner firms should engage in the balanced development of symmetric relationships where a repetitive sequence of negotiation, commitment and execution stages takes place over time and a positive assessment of three dimensions (equity, adaptability, efficiency) encourages them to make irreversible commitments. This represents the first of potentially numerous learning cycles. As the relationship achieves an efficiency gain, the partners are willing to make additional commitments that would end up improving the efficiency of the alliance further, thus leading to a sequence of learning cycles with associated higher performance.

More specifically, the competitive analysis is appropriate in cases where excess profits of an incumbent alliance result from limitations on the intensity of internal rivalry (that is, competition within an industry) achieved via raising structural or strategic entry barriers, reducing the threat of substitute products and/or being the price-setter with suppliers and customers. A purely external view on alliance strategy is thus based on the identification of structural industry attractiveness and subsequently on the acquisition of the requisite assets. However, such a pure external view does not provide a strong foundation for the formulation of a dynamic, long-term alliance strategy in volatile markets where customer preferences and technologies tend to change rapidly.

The resource-based view of the firm has a different orientation. It looks at excess profits as arising from specific resources and capabilities within the firm and its potential collaborations with other companies. It thus tends to implement a value-creating strategy aimed at creating distinctive and inimitable advantages. Alliances with a specific strategic value are formed when each partner firm contributes its own resource position to the cooperative venture making it more difficult for competitors to replicate and catch up. According to the RBV, the establishment of a corporate competitive advantage at individual/company or alliance level requires exploiting and constantly developing firm-specific capabilities.

The dynamic capabilities approach emphasizes not only how organizations first develop firm-specific capabilities, but also how they renew their competencies to react to rapid changes of the business environment. Based on this theory, value-augmenting strategic change is difficult and costly, and it generally occurs incrementally. Hence, distinctive competences and capabilities cannot be acquired, but must be built over time. The implication is that a certain alliance strategy equates (e.g., for alliance partners) to choosing among and committing to long-term paths or trajectories of competence development. A competence-building strategy is path or history-dependent. It mainly depends on the policies pursued and experiences acquired in earlier periods. The chosen path not only determines which investment alternatives are open to the alliance now, but also constrains the partner firms' choices in the future. Excess profits derive not just from the cooperative venture's asset base and its degree of distinctiveness, but also from the ability of contributing partners to reconfigure and transform themselves and in turn their collaborative arrangement. The capacity of a firm to reconfigure and transform itself arises from an internal learning process and must be thus considered as a learned organizational skill.

When the external environment is in a state of flux, the adaptive resources contributed by each partner firm to a new collaborative venture and the corporate growth options these resources can generate should form a better basis for alliance strategy formulation. In line with the RBV, strategic growth options should be exercised with reference to the competences and capabilities that the alliance has relative to its competitors. Hence, management of partner firms should be able to analyze their own unique resources and capabilities individually contributed to the cooperative venture as this may better identify those strategic options that are more likely to be available to the alliance as a unique and distinctive entity compared with its competitors. Consistently with the DCV, an alliance strategy can be viewed as a series of long-term, partly irreversible commitments to certain domains of competence, which is similar to a chain of interrelated strategic (compound-like) options whose exercise accumulates resources over time and generates new opportunities in an uncertain environment. The effects of options' exercise typically overcome the boundaries of the alliance involving parent firms and are extended over time. The strategic trajectory of competence development chosen by each alliance ends up influencing the extent to which it will be successful or not.

In light of the above, options thinking in strategic alliance-making enables an explicit quantification of alliance strategy under uncertainty. We believe that an options analysis can contribute to framing and solving complex alliance problems arising in a uncertain economic environment by recognizing that each partner firm's internal resources and external strategic position to capture new market opportunities are strongly interrelated. Hence, partner firms that in establishing and running an alliance make use of their adaptable internal (tangible and intangible) resources to exploit external opportunities along favorable competence-building paths, while limiting investment and losses along unfavorable trajectories of capability development, are more likely to gain competitive advantages and experience long-term growth.

Our real options-based framework for designing, managing and appraising strategic alliances presents three key advantages over existing strategic analysis tools. First, because of the presence of inter-partner and inter-temporal growth synergies within a single alliance and among alliances run by a certain parent company, a portfolio planning approach is carefully adopted with some improvements. In a volatile business environment, alliance portfolio strategies must be flexible to enable partner firms to adjust to an uncertain and rapidly changing competitive and technological landscape. Our options analysis of alliance-making combines the best features of traditional strategic assessment tools, such as the BCG growth-share matrix, with modern valuation tools developed in corporate finance as an implementation of real options theory. A real options approach may better reveal the value of managerial flexibility in an alliance portfolio strategy when uncertainty dominates. The scope and/or outcome of the core business activity in a strategic alliance (or the business activity itself) can be viewed as a real option and as a necessary link in generating other strategic options, thus leading to cross-partner growth-driving synergistic effects within and among alliances that extend over a long-term horizon.

Second, our approach offers a dynamic valuation of alliance strategy that encompasses NPV analysis as a special case and incorporates the value of real options arising from management of evolving cooperative ventures. It represents an alternative methodology for estimating the *real* performance of a strategic partnership if compared to other more conventional appraisal tools, such as cost-benefit analysis and DCF.

Finally, a real options analysis of alliances enables one or multiple partner firms to identify and activate both the entry and the exit strategy when the collaboration is initially launched and start-up positions with associated individual contributions need to be agreed upon or it comes to an end and needs to be evenly dissolved. In this respect, case studies 1 and 2 illustrate how to apply our proposed real options framework to value and choose the right strategy to exit or enter an alliance respectively. Case study 2 provides an in-depth real options-based analysis of the bidding decision-making process undertaken by Chevron to seek to enter an alliance with Petroleos de Venezuela in the context of the bidding round arranged by the Venezuela's Ministry of Energy and Petroleum for the development of the Orinoco Belt's oil fields in 2010. Case study 1 on the joint-venture agreement signed between General Motors and Fiat in 2000 and abruptly terminated in 2005 discusses and reveals the value-added use of option clauses in the design of strategic inter-firm collaborations.

We propose a dynamic view of inter-firm collaborations that disciplines the acceptable normative prescriptions provided by the theory of strategic management via a more rigorous analytical process to help alliance managers cultivate and exploit long-run adaptive flexibility and, as a result, create and sustain competitive advantage.

Part II
Case Studies

Chapter 7
Assessing Strategic Alliances in Bad Times: The Case of General Motors—Fiat

Abstract Case study 1 illustrates how to apply our proposed real options framework to value and choose the right strategy to exit strategic alliances. More specifically, the case study presented here on the joint-venture agreement signed between General Motors and Fiat in 2000 and abruptly terminated in 2005 discusses and reveals the value-added use of option clauses in the design of strategic inter-firm collaborations.

Keywords Shared-supply alliance • Joint-venture agreement • Automotive sector • Operating synergies • Put option • Binomial tree

On March 13, 2000 General Motors (GM) and Fiat formed a strategic alliance of shared-supply type signing a joint-venture (JV) agreement based on the motto "allies in costs, competitors in the markets". In a globalized automotive sector in which U.S. automakers lost more than 20 % of their market share to Japanese and other competitors, the deal was critically important for GM. Fiat Auto's divisions (Fiat, Alfa Romeo, Lancia) also experienced a significant market share erosion in Italy and Western Europe. The Agnelli family's psychological commitment to the auto business and fear of losing control led them to forego any deal with European auto makers. Only a partnership involving a high degree of autonomy for the Agnelli family could provide new growth opportunities and partial protection against market uncertainty. Although being the world largest automaker with financial resources to acquire Fiat or engage in other M&As, GM was fast losing competitive position and experiencing losses in certain geographic areas including Europe (Opel). The deal was designed to capture the benefits of managerial flexibility embedded in a JV in a dynamically changing environment, including enhancement of respective competitive positions, the transfer of organizational knowledge, costs savings and resolution of "endogenous" uncertainty over the partner's capabilities via a mutual staged learning process.

The GM-Fiat strategic alliance was by design symmetric to avoid giving the perception of an acquisition by GM disguised as a JV agreement. The equity of the resulting two JV entities on the main areas of the partnership (purchasing and powertrain)—GM-Fiat Worldwide Purchasing B.V. and Fiat-GM

F. Baldi, *Options in Alliances*, SpringerBriefs in Business,
DOI: 10.1007/978-88-470-2850-0_7,

Powertrain B.V.—was divided 50/50 among the parties with the two new entities having a chairman appointed by GM and a CEO appointed by Fiat and vice versa. The first entity focused on worldwide purchasing to achieve cost reduction and product quality enhancement through a centralized reorganization of parts and component purchasing activities, their rationalization based on common design of powertrains and a greater bargaining power with suppliers due to combined purchasing volumes. The second new entity was formed to manufacture engines and gearboxes exploiting the scale and scope of economies from integrated development of a new knowledge base for the more complex parts of the vehicle based on use of a special architecture. This would enable synergies from manufacturing common components and systems in large quantities while maintaining the specific features of each brand. The overall operating synergies expected from the deal were about $2.0 billion. The combination of such prospective synergistic savings and growth opportunities from shared purchasing and powertrain manufacturing activities (e.g., supplying other automakers) accounted for almost 80 % of the manufacturing cost of a vehicle.

The alliance was geographically limited to Europe and South-America. Although GM did not suffer significant competitive pressures in the North-American market, Europe was facing increasingly fiercer competition. The Latin American market was considered to embed growth opportunities. The new entity emerging from this strategic alliance involving integration of the activities of GM in Europe and Latin America and Fiat Auto would be ranked fifth globally with the cooperation limited to upstream activities (downstream activities were kept autonomous). The alliance also entailed some degree of cooperation in financial services.

From a financial standpoint, GM swapped 6 % of its shares for 20 % of Fiat shares at a purchase price of $2.4 billion. The equity swap was not closed at market prices but was rather based on the estimated values of each parties' branches conferred to the new entity. The resulting implied equity value of Fiat was $12.0 billion (below its then market capitalization of $16.3 billion). Fiat thus became GM's second-largest shareholder and its main industrial partner with ability to fund new initiatives of corporate restructuring and equity capital strengthening. According to usual JV practice, GM could ask for an expansion (call-like) option to acquire more of Fiat in case of a success and an abandonment (put-like) option to sell back its initial investment in case of a failing partnership. Instead, GM opted to grant Fiat a put option in compensation for the "unfair" conditions of the equity swap. In doing so, GM assumed that the value of Fiat would not drop significantly due to the realization of the above operating synergies and that the Italian government would not agree to the sell off this key national automotive group. The put option clause gave Fiat the right to oblige GM to buy the remaining 80 % of the automotive business unit in the next 4–9 years (following a "black-out period" in the first 4 years) at an exercise price to be fairly determined by three financial institutions.

Unfortunately, the market fortunes of Fiat (and GM) took a downturn and within 5 years this put option to force purchase of Fiat Auto turned around to haunt GM. By 2002 Fiat's record losses forced a restructuring program under pressure from its creditor banks involving the sale of Fidis (consumer credit) and Toro Assicurazioni (insurance) to reduce outstanding debt and recapitalize the company. At the time GM was overwhelmed by other problems, such as skyrocketing US health-care costs, and had neither the excess funds nor the desire to acquire the residual 80 % stake in Fiat. GM instead claimed Fiat violated the put contract by recapitalizing the company and selling its 51 % stake in Fidis, thereby halving GM's stake in Fiat and nullifying the cooperation in financial services. In December 2004 the top managements of GM and Fiat met at Lake Konstanz to reach a compromise on the execution of the put option and access the financial implications if GM decided to exercise or opt out of it. Although the meeting ended without an announced agreement, soon thereafter (on February 13, 2005) GM and Fiat announced they had agreed to nullify the put option and dissolve their 5-year partnership. GM agreed to pay Fiat \$2.0 billion in cash for cancelling the put option and dissolving the partnership. In this way, GM would avoid having to acquire the loss-making auto business unit of Fiat and being stuck with \$5.3 billion in debt and pension obligations for tens of thousands of aging Italian workers. GM returned its equity interest in Fiat Auto to Fiat.

What was the put option embedded in the GM-Fiat JV agreement really worth at the time of the dissolution agreement on February 13, 2005? Was the \$2.0 billion payment by GM to cancel the put option and exit the partnership in line with the operating synergies prospects and unfulfilled obligations resulting from the option clause (cancellation)? Below we illustrate how to value the put option embedded in the GM-Fiat strategic alliance using the standard binomial option model (Cox et al. 1979; Trigeorgis 1996).

The underlying asset of the put option involves (selling) the remaining 80 % claim on Fiat's equity value. At the time of the dissolution agreement on February 13, 2005 this had an estimated market capitalization value of \$4.48 billion. This underlying value (V) is assumed to follow a multiplicative binomial process, moving up by a multiplicative factor u or down by d each year. The up and down factors determine the range of future values (driven by Fiat's stock volatility) and are estimated as follows:

$$\mathrm{u} = e^{\sigma\sqrt{\Delta t}} = e^{0.37\sqrt{1}} = 1.45 \qquad \mathrm{d} = 1/\mathrm{u} = 0.69.$$

Fiat equity's annual volatility based on Fiat's historical daily prices over the previous 5-year period was estimated at 37 % ($\sigma = 0.37$) and the time subinterval (Δt) is 1 year. The risk-free interest rate, based on the yield on 10-year Treasury Notes, was about 4 % ($r = 0.04$). The above (uV and dV) and follow-on states of nature can be reached with risk neutral probabilities p_u and p_d ($= 1 - p_u$) estimated from

$$p_u = \frac{(1+r)-d}{u-d} = \frac{(1+0.04)-0.69}{1.45-0.69} = 0.46.$$

These probabilities ($p_u = 0.46$ and $p_d = 0.54$) are constant throughout the binomial tree and can be used to determine the (risk-adjusted) expected value of the put option's future payoffs, that are subsequently discounted at the risk free rate (r). The put option's remaining life as of February 13, 2005 (following the

Table 7.1 Evolution of underlying asset value (V): 80 % equity stake in Fiat on February 13, 2005

				$19.68
			$13.59	
		$9.39		$9.39
	$6.49		$6.49	
$4.48		$4.48		$4.48
	$3.09		$3.09	
		$2.14		$2.14
			$1.48	
				$1.02
0	1	2	3	4
2005	*2006*	*2007*	*2008*	*2009*

V in $ billions

4-year blackout period) until expiration in 2009 is 4 years (was 9 years at the initial purchase of the 20 % equity stake in Fiat in 2000). The stochastic evolution of the underlying asset (80 % equity stake in Fiat), V, is given in Table 7.1.

If the exercise price of the put option (X), namely the fair purchase price of the remaining 80 % of Fiat Auto's equity determined at the time of the actual exercise (February 2005) is assumed for simplicity to remain constant at $4.48 billion, the put option's payoff at maturity is P = max(X − V, 0) or max(4.48 − V, 0), given in the last column in the second (option) tree below. For example, in the bottom right state, P^d = max(4.48 − 1.02, 0) = 3.46, whereas in the state just above it, P^u = max(4.48 − 2.14, 0) = 2.34. In all higher states the put option is not worth exercising (receiving 0). In the lower state one period earlier (at t = 3 in 2008) the option is worth (a continuation value):

$$\frac{\left[p_u * P^u + p_d * P^d\right]}{(1+r)} = \frac{\left[0.46 * 2.34 + 0.54 * 3.46\right]}{1.04} = 2.83.$$

Being an option of American type that can be exercised at any time (between 2005 and 2009), the above continuation option value (computed as the expected value of the follow-on state-of-nature payoffs discounted back one period) must be compared to the current payoff from early exercise at each step in a backward induction process. In the lowest state in 2008, the then exercise value is X − V = 4.48 − 1.48 = 3.00. This early exercise value exceeds the above option

Table 7.2 Option value estimates for the GM-Fiat put option

				$0.00
			$0.00	
		$0.00		$0.00
	$0.37		$0.00	
$0.96		$0.72		$0.00
	$1.53		**$1.39**	
		$2.34		**$2.34**
			$3.00	
				$3.46
0	1	2	3	4
2005	*2006*	*2007*	*2008*	*2009*

V in $ billions

continuation value of 2.83 and prevails (the tree values at the corresponding nodes leading to option exercise are boldfaced). A similar process is followed for each state in each period as we move backward step by step toward year 0 (2005). Table 7.2 shows the calculated option values at each step.

The boldface numbers indicate where Fiat will exercise its put option. The put option is worth $0.96 or about $1.0 billion at the time of the dissolution of the alliance on February 13, 2005. This is about half the $2.0 billion payment GM made to Fiat at the time. The difference of another $billion might be a fair compensation for the half of the originally anticipated $2.0 billion in operating synergies that now Fiat will lose due to the dissolution of the entire partnership agreement (beyond cancellation of the put option clause part). GM may also have rationalized the $2.0 billion payment partly by avoiding to take over a loss making Fiat operation and potentially inheriting $5.4 billion in pension and other liabilities. If the GM-Fiat put option story is considered in light of recent events regarding the US automakers, it is a real paradox. History is full of ironies and reversals. GM could have bought Fiat in 2005. If it did so, its rival Chrysler might be under today. Instead, GM paid $2.0 billion to Fiat for the put option that Fiat used to strengthen its financial position. By the end of the put option expiration, in 2009, Fiat was in a strong position to come back and "rescue" GM's rival, Chrysler. Following the recent financial and economic turmoil, the Italian group has recently signed an alliance with Chrysler entailing the gradual "callable" acquisition of the US automaker at a "salvage" value. The money cashed from GM's freely-granted put option now gets exchanged into call options to rescue and gradually potentially acquire GM's main US rival!

References

Cox J, Ross SA, Rubinstein M (1979) Option pricing: a simplified approach. J Financ Econ 7:229–263

Trigeorgis L (1996) Real options. Managerial flexibility and strategy in resource allocation. MIT Press, Boston

Chapter 8
Bidding for a Strategic Alliance in Good Times: The Case of Chevron—Petroleos de Venezuela S.A.

Abstract Case study 2 illustrates how to apply our proposed real options framework to value and choose the right strategy to enter strategic alliances. More specifically, the case study presented here provides an in-depth real options-based analysis of the bidding decision-making process undertaken by Chevron to seek to enter an alliance with Petroleos de Venezuela in the context of the bidding round arranged by the Venezuela's Ministry of Energy and Petroleum for the development of the Orinoco Belt's oil fields in 2010.

Keywords Proven oil reserves • Oil bid round • Auction • Joint-venture • Call option

Venezuela is an important player in the global oil market, being among the top ten oil producers in the world. The country had 99.4 billion barrels of proven oil reserves in 2010, the largest amount in South America (*source*: Oil and Gas Journal) and, in 2008 Venezuela was the eighth-largest net oil exporter in the world. The oil sector is of central importance to the local economy accounting for more than three-quarters of total Venezuelan export revenues, about 50 % of total government revenues, and around one-third of the country's GDP.

Venezuela nationalized its oil industry in the 1970s, creating Petroleos de Venezuela S.A. (PdVSA), the country's state-run oil and natural gas company. After re-opening the upstream oil operations to private investments in the 1990s (the so called "apertura") with the creation of 32 service agreements operated by a non-PdVSA entity, such collection of policies and initiatives was largely undone in most recent years. As a result, PdVSA started both retaining the majority stake in all oil projects and demanding for higher royalty rates (along with tax burdens) on new projects. This policy was unfortunately counterproductive as the annual production declined steadily due to: (1) the maturity of most oil fields, which requires heavy investments to maintain current capacity; (2) the need for upgrading the locally produced oil that is heavy in impurities (according to international standards), contains high levels of sulfur and is hard to refine; (3) the permanent damage to PdVSA's production capacity and human capital following the strike of nearly half of company's employees (with subsequent layoffs of 18,000 workers)

F. Baldi, *Options in Alliances*, SpringerBriefs in Business,
DOI: 10.1007/978-88-470-2850-0_8,

against the nationalization process initiated by President Chavez as soon as he assumed power in 1999. In particular, the new nationalization of the country's key industries (with considerable effects on those assets locally operated by multinational firms) increased the uncertainty of doing business in Venezuela.

Faced with a decline in oil revenues and a dearth of foreign investments, it became quite evident to the government that Venezuela would have needed the expertise of foreign petrol companies to avoid heading down such a disastrous path. As a result, the government shifted strategy by awarding concessions to Western oil companies, starting up numerous joint-ventures with international partners and establishing four strategic associations (with PdVSA as a dominant partner within an international consortium) to exploit the billions of barrels of extra-heavy crude oil and bitumen deposits situated in the Orinoco Belt in central Venezuela. With the aim of further developing the region's oil resources (one of the world's largest recoverable oil reserves) in the coming years, PdVSA began a certification program to increase the amount of proven oil reserves held by the country (50 billion barrels of new reserves certified as of 2008). In this context, in October 2008 the government launched the Carabobo Bid Round, the first major oil bid round held under President Chavez. The round included the extra heavy oil reserves in the Orinoco Belt under the process of certification and specifically focused on three projects. PdVSA would take a majority stake in each project including integrated upstream and upgraded facilities with the role of overseeing crude production. The bidding procedure faced repeated delays and of the 52 companies that the Venezuelan government invited to bid, only 19 paid for field data. Several foreign oil companies opted not to bid in the auction due to the dominant political risk (and some others, such as the American companies, Exxon-Mobil and ConocoPhillips, had already left the country after the new nationalization wake). Chevron, instead, made a bid leading a group of companies in the hope of getting access to such an underdeveloped area.

The general framework of the bidding round arranged by the Venezuela's Ministry of Energy and Petroleum for the development of the Orinoco Belt's oil fields is summarized in Fig. 8.1. First, the Ministry would launch the tender offer for the granting of the mineral rights associated with the oil reservoirs discovered in the region. To participate in the round and make an official bid, each international consortium (including the one led by Chevron) would present a joint bidding agreement (JBA) signed by all internal members (1). Second, the winning consortium (which, in this case, happened to be the Chevron-led one, also including Japan's Mitsubishi and Inpex, and Venezuela's Suelopetrol) would sign a host government contract (HGC) with the State oil company (in this case, PDVSA) that is entitled to run the oil business under a natural monopolistic regime (2). For the members of the winning consortium to intrude into such a natural monopoly, they must enter a joint operating agreement (JOA) that would allow them to develop the oil field exploiting the State's license. Third, the Ministry would grant the mineral rights embedded in the oil reservoirs to the international consortium that, having made the highest bid, wins at the government's auction (3). The resulting "concession regime" would allow the State oil company and the members of the

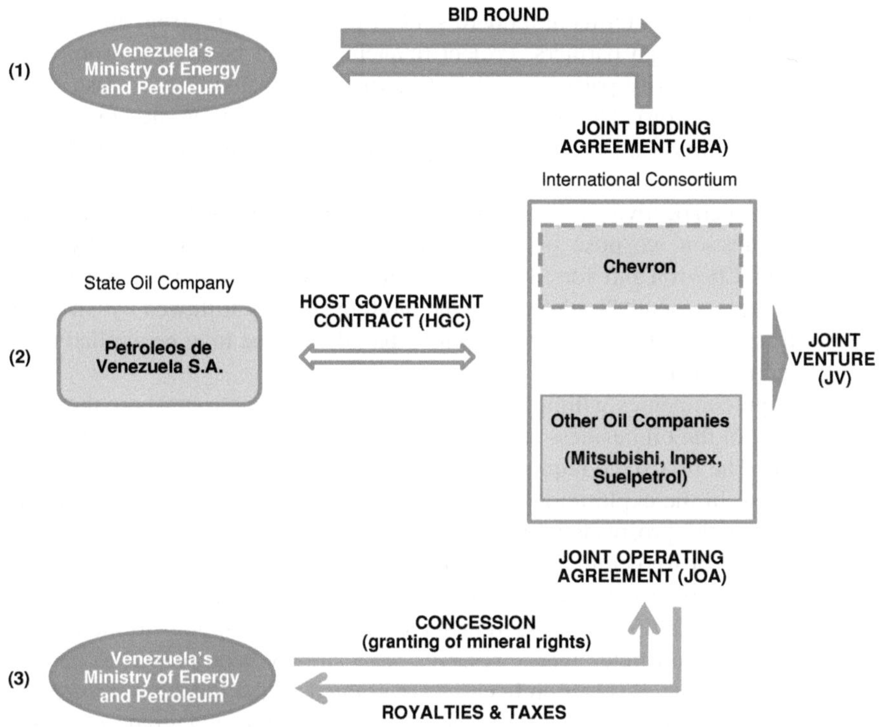

Fig. 8.1 The general framework of the oil bidding round in Venezuela (Orinoco Belt, 2008–2010)

international consortium to form a joint-venture. The consortium would be obliged to pay royalties on oil revenues and taxes to the State oil company in exchange for the above mineral rights.

In February 2010, the government announced the results of the bid round. The Chevron-led consortium secured Carabobo 3. More specifically, Chevron did not win blocks or projects but rather the right to negotiate a mixed company-based deal with the Venezuela's Ministry of Energy and Petroleum. While not signing any agreements, the winning international consortium (Carabobo 1 was secured by a Repsol-led consortium; Carabobo 2 was not awarded) would have the right (but not the obligation) to negotiate more favorable terms for the signature of a joint-venture contract needed to start the associated oil reservoir development project. By accepting to form a JV under a concession regime in Venezuela, consortium partners would commit to investing in the construction of the infrastructure that consists of: (a) upgraders converting heavy crude into lighter oil for export; (b) a production center; (c) oil pipelines. For Carabobo 3, the JV-based mixed company would include PdVSA as the majority partner (60 %) and the Chevron's consortium as the minority partner (40 %), with the U.S. company having a 34 % stake, Japanese participants 5 % and Suelopetrol 1 %. Such a scheme would fulfill the government's terms of a 60/40 split of profits deriving from all ventures established with foreign partners. Project financing would be derived from three sources: 40 % (minority partners), 30 % (international loans), 30 % (cash flows from initial production). The two Carabobo projects would allow the government to boost the country's oil production bringing it to 2.9 million barrels a day by 2017.

Taking the perspective of Chevron as the leader of one of the winning consortia, the question we pose is: *to bid or not to bid?* More specifically, how much should Chevron bid for the right to enter a JV agreement offered by the Venezuelan government? To understand the bidding strategy followed by Chevron, the straightforward but powerful real options-based calculus may be applied (Cox et al. 1979; Trigeorgis 1996).

For foreign companies willing to develop reserves in countries where the natural monopoly of the oil business exists, there are two stages at which state licenses are required. The first stage requires an exploration license that is assigned after a bidding round. In the exploration stage, initial geological studies and geophysical surveys identify the prospects within a given field. Test and appraisal drillings are done in order to prove economically exploitable reserves. The exploration license conveys an exclusive right to explore the field for a certain period of time. If the above tests are successful, a production stage follows. This applies to the case of the Orinoco Belt's oil fields whose reserves have already been proved to be economically exploitable. Production licenses are granted by the local government (in this case, the Venezuela's Ministry of Energy and Petroleum) via a bidding procedure for a given period of time (e.g., 20 years). The winning leading company (and its consortium), Chevron, is entitled to request a production license (or concession) for the development of the fields under the name of Carabobo 3. Normally, it takes several years to build capacity (in terms of drilling wells, storage, transport facilities, etc.) before starting production. As this stage requires the largest capital expenditures, this is where option value becomes most important. Based on the potential granting of a production license, Chevron's management must determine whether and when it is optimal to invest in exploitation facilities, given the quantity of reserves (estimated according to the production profile for the field's useful life) and the uncertainty of oil prices.

The Venezuelan government's receipts from entering a JV with Chevron and its partners consist of: (i) royalties (16 %); (ii) profit share via direct participation (60 %); (iii) corporate income tax (80 %). More specifically, the country's new fiscal regime on oil revenues of foreign companies provides that a tax rate of 80 % is applied when the oil price rises above \$70, with the taxation level increasing to 90 and 95 % when prices exceed \$90 and \$100 respectively. Because the average WTI price for the 6 months-period preceding the valuation date (January 2, 2010) is \$72, the applicable tax rate is 80 %. In exchange for these payments, Chevron enters a JV that exploits a reservoir producing 400,000 barrels of crude oil per day over a 20 year-lifetime (with start in 2014). Such a pace of production will be maintained for the first 4 years and will successively decline by 10 % every year. The price for the extra-heavy crude oil extracted from the Orinoco region is typically discounted at 20 % over the WTI (West Texas Intermediate, a type of light crude used as a benchmark in oil pricing and underlying commodity of oil future contracts traded at NYMEX). Yet, the price considered in the Chevron's business plan is \$71 (the 5-year average price over the 2005–2009 period). As the low quality of such oil demands a higher cost to extract, process and transport, operational expenditures are estimated at \$9/bbl and capital expenditures are equal to about \$4.16 billion. The high country risk demands a 30 % cost of capital, which accounts for country risk (much higher than the 10 % discount rate typically used, according to the SEC criteria, for reservoir valuations associated with companies listed at NYSE).

Chevron's offer is structured as follows: (1) \$500 million as a bonus payment (or signing fee), of which \$100 million due upon signing the documents to form a mixed company and the other four equal installments in the course of oil development (before the start of exploitation); (2) \$1 billion as a financing of the project. In exchange for contributing to the financing of the project, Chevron would be granted a physical stock of 300 million barrels of crude for 7 years (2014–2020) for export purposes as a dividend payment.

The strategic alliance that PDVSA (majority partner) and Chevron (leading minority partner) may potentially form is horizontal complementary as it allows the U.S. company to access oil reservoirs in Venezuela through the privilege of a government concession in exchange for upgrading the local facilities for their development. The latter would not have gained such exploitation rights without the openness strategy implemented by the Venezuelan government through its state-owned oil company and the former would have not been able to efficiently exploit its own fields without Chevron's willingness to share its own knowledge and expertise in upstream operations. Viewing the partnership through option lens, the PDVSA-Chevron alliance—if the latter decides to incur the associated investment cost of \$1.5 billion—would give the U.S. company not only the right to co-exploit a mineral extraction concession in Venezeula but also to expand its export volumes via value appropriation expected from physical dividend payments. Based on real options theory, Chevron must bid for the concession right including the value of the call-like option to expand the scope of the alliance beyond the domestic Venezuelan market due to the grant of extra, upgraded crude that the U.S. company can take to the market on a stand-alone basis. The exercise price of such a call option corresponds to Chevron's offer for the bidding round.

Based on the following parameters:

- risk free rate (r) = 4.6 %;
- 2005–2009 WTI (historical, annualized) price volatility (σ) = 44.2 %;
- binomial upward factor (u) = 1.56;
- binomial downward factor (d) = 0.64;
- risk-neutral probabilities = 0.44 (p_u) and 0.56 (p_d);
- mean reversion coefficient (k) for WTI prices (2005–2008) = \$4.6.

Two are the real options-based approaches (alternative to naïve NPV analysis) that can be followed to set an optimal bid for the Carabobo 3's JV. We call them valuation 1 and 2. Valuation 1 (more complex) calculates the expanded NPV by adding the value of the call option embedded in the JV to the passive NPV from the Chevron's business plan under the base-case scenario (−$315 million). More specifically, the expanded NPV of the Carabobo 3's JV is calculated by pricing at year t = 20 an American call option whose payoff takes the following form:

$$\textbf{call option} = \text{Max}\,[CF_t - exercise\ price; 0]$$

where:

$$CF_t = [(1 - R) * JV\ share * P_{\text{export}} * (1 - discount) * oil\ output - opex] * (1 - tax\ rate) + P_{\text{export}} * oil\ grant$$

with CF_t = cash flow at time t; R = royalty rate = 16 %; *JV share* = 34 %; P_{export} = oil price for export = $91.86 (WTI future contract with January 2014 delivery, as traded as of January 1, 2010); *discount* = discount on current WTI price for extra-heavy crude = 20 %; *oil output* = yearly amount of oil produced (in bbl) = 146 million; *opex* = operational expenditures = $9/bbl * *oil output*; *tax rate* = 80 %; *oil grant* = amount of physical dividend payment in barrels of crude = 32 % of 300 million barrels on a yearly basis (granted over the 2014–2020 period and exportable at non-discounted prices).

$$exercise\ price = \text{bonus (signing fee)} + \text{equity financing} = \$1.5\ \text{billion}$$

and by then choosing recursively in a backward induction fashion (at all previous years) the maximum amount between the current value of the above payoff and the present value of future, residual cash flows from keeping the option open for one more period. This yields an expanded NPV of about $2.5 billion.

Valuation 2 (simpler) combines the passive NPV from the Chevron's business plan under the export scenario ($1.1 billion) including the oil grant as a dividend payment with the stand-alone value of the call-like option exercisable by Chevron to receive the above grant ($2.2 billion). More specifically, such a right is assigned to Chevron if management decides to incur the investment cost of the bonus plus the equity financing. The payoff of such a call option (of American type) is:

$$\textbf{call option} = \text{Max}\,[CF_t - exercise\ price; 0]$$

where:

$$CF_t = P_{\text{export}} * oil\ grant$$

The expanded NPV is equal to about $3.2 billion.

As a result, the range of option values embedded in the expanded NPV of the Chevron's venture in Venezuela is $2.2 billion (valuation 2) to $2.8 billion (valuation 1). Bringing to the surface (and appraising) those real options that allow to manage a JV more flexibly is valuable as it yields a dynamic NPV of about $2.5 billion, which is almost 2.5 times the passive one ($1.1 billion). The key difference between the two is that, under a passive NPV analysis, the export revenues potentially accruable to Chevron are statically inserted in the business plan, while, if a real options valuation is performed, they are considered as the payoff of a call option-like right granted to the U.S. company due to the fact that the venture is formed. Both options are American as Chevron may decide to start operations only if and when it is optimal to do so.

Conclusively, it seems that Chevron will extract synergies from allying with PDVSA that are associated with output expansion (beyond the scope of the alliance located in Venezuela) in its other international markets and more than repay the rigid fee (including equity) due upon establishment of the JV. If the venture is *actively* managed seeking to capture the value of crude price uncertainty as it resolves over time, bidding for a partnership with the Venezuelan state-owned oil company at $1.5 billion is more than optimal!

References

Cox J, Ross SA, Rubinstein M (1979) Option pricing: a simplified approach. J Financ Econ 7:229–263

Trigeorgis L (1996) Real options. Managerial flexibility and strategy in resource allocation. MIT Press, Boston

MIX
Papier aus verantwortungsvollen Quellen
Paper from responsible sources
FSC® C105338

If you have any concerns about our products,
you can contact us on
ProductSafety@springernature.com

In case Publisher is established outside the EU,
the EU authorized representative is:
Springer Nature Customer Service Center GmbH
Europaplatz 3, 69115 Heidelberg, Germany

Printed by Libri Plureos GmbH
in Hamburg, Germany